# 5 BLINDERS TO
# SEEING COLOR

*Angela "Doc" Courage!, Ed.D.*
*LaTonya R. Jackson, Ed.D.*

Library of Congress Control Number: 2020919945

ISBN: 978-1-945566-13-4 (eBook)
ISBN: 978-1-945566-15-8 (paperback)

Eyedentified Consulting Services, LLC
d/b/a Eyedentified Publishing Solutions
P.O. Box 6892
Springdale, AR 72766-6892

www.seecolorr.com


Publisher's Cataloging-In-Publication Data
(Prepared by The Donohue Group, Inc.)

Names: Courage!, Angela, author. | Jackson, LaTonya R., 1978- author.
Title: 5 blinders to seeing color / Angela "Doc" Courage!, Ed.D., LaTonya
    R. Jackson, Ed.D.
Other Titles: Five blinders to seeing color
Description: 1st ed. | Springdale, AR : Eyedentified Publishing Solutions,
    LLC, [2020] | Includes bibliographical references.
Identifiers: ISBN 9781945566158 (paperback) | ISBN 9781945566134 (ebook)
Subjects: LCSH: Race awareness. | Race relations. | Intercultural
    communication. | Race discrimination.
Classification: LCC HT1521 .C68 2020 (print) | LCC HT1521 (ebook) | DDC
    305.8--dc23

# WHO THIS BOOK IS FOR

This book is for those who seek an inclusive perspective regarding color and culture. The content adds to the inclusion and diversity discussion given historical and cultural context with personal and professional insights from the authors. The list of those who will benefit from this book includes:

- **Leaders** who seek to be inclusive.

- **Human Resource/People Managers or Directors** in for-profit and non-profit organizations who want to continue (or initiate) conversations that enhance inclusion and diversity

- **Senior Leaders and staff** in faith-based organizations seeking ways to discuss diversity and inclusion in their faith-context

- **College Faculty, Administrators and students** looking for programming or class conversations to improve inclusion and student experience on college campuses

- **School Administrators** who desire to help their staff engage in inclusive conversations with parents, students, and their communities more effectively

- **Public Service leaders and administrators** who seek to create connected and inclusive communities

- **Individuals** who want to grow their own knowledge and wish to contribute to the conversation without causing harm to others

# Prologue

Everywhere we look we see color. To pretend that color doesn't exist would mean that we live in a world that is colorless. In 2016, we partnered together to work on a training bid for a federal opportunity. The organization focused on the Arts and we took creative license to design a training program and model to address the cognitive, affective and behavioral learning needs that aligned to that organization's strategy. We didn't get the bid and a series of life events began to happen which included a process of Angela beating breast cancer, and a new family addition for LaTonya. The time lapse proved perfect as the series of 2020 events led to the emergence of a timely opportunity for the authors to reconnect on the project and the environment was ready to receive the work they had begun.

We want you to know that we know how to spell color. For our purposes, **COLOR²** is an acronym for Culture, Openness, Leadership, Outreach, Relationship and Results. COLOR2 is the model that we designed for the 2016 project to address the rational, emotional and behavioral needs. We wanted leadership to recall, reinforce and relive experiences garnered through creative lenses to facilitate connection and communication. In our discovery, and following the 2016 election, we began to learn and hear people express angst over the results. The phrase "I don't see color" became a more prominent statement. As racial tensions have escalated, it became more important to bring awareness and understanding of the impact of those words to the conversation.

We looked at each other and decided that the work we had done to create The C.O.L.O.R.2 Expressions program was not in vain. In fact, what we actually said is, "we've almost got a book"! Then as we began working on the book, we decided an introductory eBook would help us to get the information out quicker.

We invite you to read this book and then join share your thoughts with us at https://www.facebook.com/groups/seecolorr/. There we will be further opportunity to build on what you have gained from this book including more details on the The C.O.L.O.R.2 Expressions program.

So take a look at your surroundings – take note of the color you see as you engage and read *5 Blinders to Seeing COLOR²*!

# Dedication

*This book is dedicated to those who desire to see more clearly how to change our color blindness into cultural sightedness.*

# Contents

# Acknowledgements

We have a heart of gratitude to all who have been on this journey with us. We are blessed beyond measure to have you rooting us on!

To the one who created us, may He be glorified in this work and all that we do.

To our husbands who see, support and work towards the vision of conciliation as hard as we do.

To our generational legacy, may they be seen and appreciated in the world for who they are, in their multiple colors and cultures, from pink, to brown and black, all beautiful.

To our mentors who listened and shared their wisdom with us. We would not be here without them.

To our graphic designer, Klressa Barnes Creations, for this amazing cover design that captures our readers before they open the pages.

To our editor, Holly Holt, who helped proofread, edit and encourage the work that we're doing by sharing it with her loved ones.

# 1

# INTRODUCTION

Have you ever heard or perhaps maybe you've said one of the following statements?

*"I don't see color."*

*"I see everyone the same."*

*"We don't see color because we love everyone."*

*"We love everyone."*

Each of these statements is precisely why this book was written and we are so excited that you've chosen to take this journey to grow beyond your current knowledge of color and culture barriers as we share ways to remedy color blindness.

Our aim with this book is to help each reader recognize cultural blinders so they can see color and respect culture, enabling more effective communication and connection to build and/or enhance every kind of human relationship. Here are the potential benefits of seeing color:

- Reduce stress and anxiety around cultural communication

- Improve confidence about culturally appropriate dialogue
- Increase capacity to negotiate uncertain contexts
- Become equipped to navigate race and color conversations
- Gain tools to minimize unintentional offense

We encourage you to take the time to learn more about the members of your community who have cultural, generational, socioeconomic, ethnic, or international experiences and perspectives that you have not yet learned. We also encourage you to make the time to become informed and fluent when communicating across culture and color lines. As a result of engaging in these actions, you have the potential to become a catalyst in your corporation, community, or religious expression that helps create positive change and moves the conversation forward beyond rhetoric and suggesting blame.

This book augments the information available within the inclusion and diversity industry and offers a fresh perspective on enhancing cultural understanding, and communication in relationships among diverse individuals and groups of people.

In order to change our current color blindness into cultural sightedness we must choose to learn to see color and culture and be willing to appreciate their importance in the journey to overcome racial inequity, privilege and systemic concerns. There's no way around it, without making a conscious intentional choice to see color we are creating a barrier that limits our profitability, restrains creativity, hinders relationships, minimizes teamwork, stifles courage, and restricts vision because of refusing to "see color."

We all have a background or heritage and building relationships are the best way to learn and subsequently respect the differences that we each value and bring to each other. Let's work together to eliminate excuses to hide or retreat when the topic of color, culture, and race come up in a conversation.

## ABOUT COLOR AND RACE

We know there is no significant biological difference between people who have been categorized as different "races." As a matter of fact, research has shown there is more diversity of genes within a racial category than there is between people of different racial categories. "Race" was a construction of categories (social construct) used to define how we rank social order in the United States of America and other colonized countries. As such, this man-made hierarchy created a pyramid where groups at the top were given more power and other groups lower in the pyramid were given less power. This hierarchical structure was made to be a color caste system for the purpose of maintaining power based on Western European traditions of culture, conquest, and religious expression.

Based on our racialized histories and what European colonizers, immigrants, and their descendants were socialized to believe from early childhood, it has been thought by those in power (primarily white males) to be in everyone's best interest to maintain the pyramid and the power as it had been designed despite the constitutional mantra and national rhetoric that all men are created equal.

Recall the timeframe when "all men are created equal" was penned: In America, Black people and women were not among those groups for whom equal rights were being considered. In fact, Black people were only considered ¼ - ⅗ human depending on the colony or state. We know that historically the people who penned those words did not intend "all men" to mean all people. This mantra excluded women and any person who possessed one drop of blood from Africa. There was an implicit understanding and it was the accepted cultural norm given the time in which the statement was written.

In fact, Thomas Jefferson, the one who wrote the words, "all men are created equal" personally reflected the context of that historical period in our history. The evidence to support this has been well documented, given that he not only owned people of African descent (called slaves) but used his power and position of authority to impregnate his "slaves" against their will. As a result, children from an unwanted relationship were born into a society where laws were against them because of the color of their mother's skin and their mother's legal state of slavery. Furthermore, the laws protected the "pyramid of white supremacy" by allowing those in power and to father children who were not considered sons or heirs to the inheritance that would have otherwise been available to them.

Black people, Native Americans, and Latinos were considered the legal property of people who purchased them for slave labor, known as "masters," most often of European descent. Those who were held captive by slavers lived with the threat of death and/or great physical harm to themselves and to their unborn or born children. They were thus not legally able to deny consent to their white "masters" for anything, including sex. They could be emasculated, castrated, sold, traded, or killed on a whim because of the color of their skin. Laws were created to ensure the legality of such transactions. Indentured servants who exchanged their freedom for passage to the "New World" were not subjected to the same conditions. There were laws passed beginning in 1620 to protect white indentured servants from the same treatment as Black indentured servants and slaves.

---

*"We need to give each the space to grow, to be ourselves, to exercise our diversity. We need to give each other space so that we may both give and receive such beautiful things as ideas, openness, dignity, joy, healing and inclusion."*

---

*~Max De Pree*

## Reflection

Were those who were perceived as white subject to this same level of treatment or systemic legal processes? Search the laws for indentured servants that were white and Black, namely the landmark precedent set in 1620 to reflect upon this question.

Most people understand the history of the Holocaust and have seen the photos of the treatment that was done there, and we've heard the stories they told and the abuses they faced. How then is it possible that the history of Blacks in America who shared a similar fate over a much longer period is not well known? Or worse, it incites such emotion that we go to extreme points of view seeking to place blame on victims and their descendants instead of taking ownership of the history that shaped the nation. Have we considered the trauma, loss, and grief of the descendants of those enslaved like we have of others?

This book's purpose is not to discount nor diminish the experiences of any other racial group; rather to help us to see beyond what we have come to believe as facts in our society. To say "I don't see color" yields the idea that the barely-known history of the person of color to whom you speak is invisible. It mutes and minimizes the reality of what their ancestors faced and much of what still exists in today's environment through lenses masked by systems using the law to continue racial disparity.

North America was not "discovered," there were already people here, it was simply annexed. However, the reason Columbus (as well as those who funded his mission and who came after him to the shores of what is now the United States of America) colonized, euthanized, and enslaved humans in the first place goes back to a belief that they (the colonizers) were created by God as superior, and that they were endowed by God to occupy and "subdue" the land and its inhabitants (manifest destiny).

The concept of "race" was non-existent until the late 1600's. In 1684, Berneir, a French physician, began to write about race. In 1785 Linneaus developed the work on classifying life forms on earth into kingdom, phylum, class, order, family, genus, and species, of which humans were assigned to the species homo sapiens. We still use this ordering system today. From 1816-1882, Arthur de

Gatineau was the first to categorize race into a hierarchy or "white, Black, and yellow" with white being (in his opinion) the "superior" race.

It was Blumenbach[i], a student of Linnaeus, that was most influential in developing the current social construct of "race," now debunked as pseudo-science, known as "Blumenbach's Geometry of Human Order[ii]" (1995). He focused on extending Linnaeus's classification system one more level beyond species into "race" of the human species. His work is what most scholars point to as the pseudo-science that was used to begin the justification of the mistreatment of humans that were not "Caucasian."

Previous categories were based on geography, not appearance or body types. Blumenbach's--as well as previous work--was also influenced by ethnocentric perceptions of his own personal ethnic group as being superior. If we consider the times when people could not easily travel or interact with counterparts in distant areas across the globe, it is easy to understand how high ethnocentrism (preference for one's own people and cultural ways) would be more the rule than the exception. Blumenbach's work claimed a hierarchal ranking with Europeans/ "Caucasians" being at the top of a pyramid, the middle occupied by "Malays and Americans" referring

---

i    Blumenbach J. (1969). On the natural varieties of mankind. (T. Bendyshe, Trans.). New York: Bergman Publishers. (Original work published 1865).

ii   Blumenbach J. (1969). On the natural varieties of mankind. (T. Bendyshe, Trans.). New York: Bergman Publishers. (Original work published 1865).

to Malaysians and Polynesians of the Pacific, aborigine of Australia. The base of the human order, Blumenbach believed, were Africans and Asians.

Every system of classification that has developed since then has essentially been built upon the assumption that Blumenbach's work was validated by scientific expertise and based primarily on physical features (phenotypes) of skin color, hair type, eye color, body type, and facial features. Using these features of implied worth, beauty, and virtue, the American legal structure, economy, and society was built. Ethnocentrism, self-serving bias, and outgroup thinking led to errors of judgment and negative attributions about the character and human value of millions of people and their cultures.

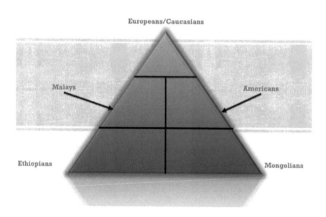

The creation of supposed "orders" of the species Homo-Sapiens led to some key beliefs that enabled the domination, exploitation, and abuse of lands and people during the colonialization period. According to Orbe &

Harris[iii], the key beliefs held by the dominant Europeans were that:

1. Humankind consisted of well-defined races.
2. Some races were superior to others.
3. The superior race should rule over the other races and that everyone benefited with Europeans as "stewards" and others becoming "civilized" and introducing them to Christianity.

It comes as no surprise that the people who designed this racial hierarchy were, in fact, at the top[iv]. This is the danger of ethnocentric belief systems.

As scientific methods have improved, and scientists from all over the world have been able to participate and scrutinize each other's methods, as well as share data, a multitude of exhaustive studies have thoroughly debunked the myth of race as subgroups in the human species. Humankind never had different "pure" orders as some "racial purists" would like to claim. Quite to the contrary, it is now understood that the whole of humanity comes from one source, Africa[v]. Our migrations over the earth have caused our bodies to adapt and evolve as needed for survival in the parts of the world where our ancestors settled.

iii   Orbe, M., Harris, T. (2015). Interracial Communication: Theory into practice (3rd ed.). Sage Publications, Thousand Oaks, CA.
iv   The word "Caucasian" comes from the region in Europe called the Caucasus Mountain region in Europe.
v    Khan Academy, Big History Project: How did the first humans live.

Blue eyes were recently discovered as a "mutation" that developed as humans migrated to extreme northern parts of the earth where there are long months of darkness at a time. Prior to that time, all humans had brown eyes. It is also now known that genetic variability is greater within groups than between groups who appear to be "racially" different.

In fact, we are not "racial" beings, we are cultural beings. We have developed cultures and ways of life based on our histories, geographies, and experiences in the world. We've been enculturated (trained by our culture) to believe that people of various hues are better or worse than one another based on skin color since before the United States came into existence. However, while skin color only gives us clues about a person, those clues may not be typical with the larger population of that cultural group, or it may. If we ignore skin color, we also ignore important parts of life that a person has likely experienced. I show up everywhere I go as a woman. People treat me differently as a woman than they would if I was a man. Some of that is not to my liking. Similarly, Black people and white people show up in the same spaces and get treated differently. Noticing each person, and giving honor to each person regardless of the ethnocentrism we have been trained to have, is what we hope to help you become stronger at as you read the rest of this book.

## "I don't see color."

Have you ever said or heard someone say, "I don't see color?" Individuals who make this statement may not be trying to dismiss people of color or their ethnic heritage. It is possible that people who make this blanket statement believe that there is no racial categorization because we all bleed red. Perhaps they are anxious or nervous around people of color due to an awareness that one is culturally unskilled, thus resulting in a heightened desire to be cautious because the interaction and person are important to them. Maybe it is an awkward attempt to show empathy or lack of exposure to the realities faced by people of color. It is even possible that a person knowingly has blatantly racist thoughts and behaviors and seeks to conceal those for fear of negative consequences to themselves without regard or concern for the person with whom they are interacting. Sometimes the statement may reveal a bias that is unknown and often referred to as implicit bias.

Here's what we believe a person is trying to say when they make the statement "I don't see color": *"While there is an obvious difference in us, you are more important to me than your skin color, and I value you as a person."* It may be intended as a compliment and represent the idea that I don't see any difference. And while this is good, it could be coupled with the idea or thought that "you're just like me." This is where concern emerges. The intention was good but the idea or thought that follows creates a barrier. The idea that they are just like you negates the history we described earlier and could lend itself to a perception of invisibility of the person of color who has historically been overlooked for everything EXCEPT his or her skin color.

How might a person of color with whom you are not connected nor have taken the time to learn to communicate perceive what is said? In many instances, the phrase "I don't see color" is generally heard as, *"In order not to treat you in a manner that acknowledges I am privileged, I need to see you as just like me because either my past experience with people of color is limited or non-existent, my exposure and engagement with people who look like you is limited to what has been portrayed in media or entertainment, your skin color triggers me, or I want to believe that I am not like them (the Ku Klux Klan); therefore, if I say I do not see your skin color, I will appear as a nice person and hopefully avoid making myself sound or appear racist or exclusive in any way."*

Or the phrase "I don't see color" could be heard as harshly as, *"In order not to treat you in a racist way, I need to pretend you are white because your skin color triggers me, or leads me to believe somewhere inside of me that you are inferior to me; therefore, if I try not to see your color, I will be nicer and hopefully avoid making myself look racist."*

The statement "I don't see color" was intended to be insightful and create trust but what happens is that the comment actually creates the reverse effect, begins the erosion of trust, and breeds insensitivity. What began as an effort toward inclusion and equality results in a lasting impact that is dismissive and relationally ignorant? In other words, miscommunication and a lack of cultural understanding prevail, widening the gap of comprehension and collaboration toward a common goal of all people being recognized for difference and given equitable treatment.

## Colorblind Statements

"Colorblind" statements (and policies) are often interpreted as covert racism. The statements seek to hide or conceal the factual reality that within the system are antiquated processes and inept accountability measures to ensure that no person, regardless of their skin color, is treated unfairly or inequitably in any way. Over time, researchers have asserted that "colorblindness is the new racism" because as a society we refuse to look at the person of color and the different ways they are treated within embedded cultural systems. We all bleed red, but how one is treated despite this fact is what creates systemic blinders.

In fact, we are not all the same under the skin. What do we mean? The language "not all the same under the skin" is meant to reference the unseen impact of experience in our physical bodies that add to the individuality or uniqueness of a person. There are physical manifestations that happen under the skin given our varied experiences. So that, even though we bleed red, we are not all the same. Our individual experiences change the way we feel, think, and react to situations and circumstances as a result.

Said differently, we each have filters due to our different experiences that cause us to formulate and produce thoughts and perceptions given the manner in which we were exposed to the situation or circumstance. Our thinking and perception resulting from our varied experience shape our world view and how we choose to navigate within it. Ignoring, diminishing, or discounting the experience of a person of color because it is not your experience supports the notion that we are colorblind and continue covert operations within our reality.

Have you ever been a witness or watched a movie of a trial in court? The witness testifies presumably to the truth as they witnessed it on behalf of whichever party has called them. When the witness is cross-examined by the opposing attorney who seeks to challenge their testimony with another, the meaning of the witness is often twisted or construed to mean another thing altogether. This feeling of cross-examination and twisting of meaning (about hairstyles, clothing, music, volume, questions, etc.) is a constant reality for individuals who think, feel, and live from a different perspective and experience than the dominant population.

In America, getting pulled over while driving by a police officer does not feel the same for people of color as it does for white people. Having an outstanding warrant for a non-violent crime could cost a person of color their life as witnessed around the world with the 8 minute and 46 second video of George Floyd pleading to be let up so he could breathe. Research and events like that of Breonna Taylor and many others demonstrate that what should be normal everyday experiences are different because of the color of one's skin. This list is not exhaustive but is designed to cause you to pause and think about your daily life activities:

- Are you able to wear your hair as you wish after being offered and accepting a job?
- Have you or your relatives been prevented from graduating because you wore a braided hairstyle under your cap?
- Are you ever told that "you should know better" as if you were a child when you were seeking coaching and mentorship on the job?
- Have you been put on the "exit" or "lacks potential" list in your career because of not getting answers needed to help you grow in your role or career?
- Have you ever been asked what it was like to work on a team with 3 minority leaders?
- Have you ever been told "you came across too strong" as a leader responsible for an organizational transformational initiative because you "had a difficult past"?

- Have you ever been attacked while jogging in your neighborhood, walking through a newly constructed home?
- Have you ever been approached as suspect while in the grocery store?
- Have you been questioned for painting the wall or doing other work outside your home?
- Have you been prevented from taking after hours appointments (appliance repair services) because it's not wise for you to go out after dark to a client's home?

We are colorblind to the systems if we are still asking people of color these types of questions. These are all 2020 incidents that have occurred for people we know personally or those who have been highlighted in news media. These events occur daily for people of color. It is here where we can clearly see that color should be seen because our feelings, perspectives, and realities are quite different.

## Reflection

What do you feel would be the result of your communication and actions, if you had to justify your intent or validate your rightful position to be in your current job, drive your kind of car, or it was assumed you didn't have the education you do on a daily basis?

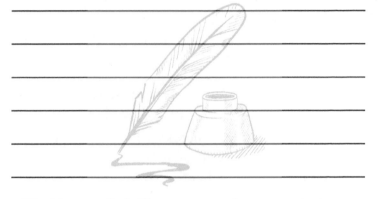

Would you feel like you are in a constant cross-examination for being born, as you are, with your hair (curly or straight, blonde, red, or brown) and with your skin (light, tan, brown, freckled, Black, or onyx) and everything that comes with daily life in the body you were born in?

## Cultural Awareness and Competence

When you go to a stop light, do you see color? Of course, you do! Red, yellow, and green. You see it and pay attention to the change of the light's color so you know how to drive according to the established laws. The color is an indicator of what to do and the action to take when the color of the light changes.

When people say they don't see color it's plausible that he or she is pretending the cultural system has no instructions for how we have decided to treat people of various ethnicities or cultures. Thus, the individual is culturally colorblind. Even the statement "I don't see color" is an indicator of cultural colorblindness. Cultural colorblindness is a choice and cultural awareness and competence is also a choice. Which will you choose?

Let's take a look at some more practical applications of the cultural colorblind concept. By seeing somebody's color (just like seeing somebody's gender, ability, or disability), it informs us of things that they have in their own personal and collective history. It informs us about how we might need to be sensitive in communicating and connecting with that person.

Meet Mr. Will, for instance. Mr. Will is a lifetime diabetic and had a stroke when he was 55, about 10 years ago. Due to complications in healing with diabetes, he now drags one foot and walks with a cane. If Mr. Will was to come to a meeting for coffee and someone pretended "ability blindness" not to see his struggle with the door, the cane and his immobile arm, it might produce unacceptable behavior such as letting the door swing, hit him, and knock him off balance. The ability-blind person might choose this behavior either intentionally or ignorantly trying not to offend Mr. Will by drawing attention to his disability. The consequences could be dire and even deadly for Mr. Will.

If unintentional, the ability-blind person might return to Mr. Will to see if he was ok and offer to assist him with getting to his meeting and maybe even buy his coffee. Whilst a person intentionally letting the door swing would do neither and might take the opportunity to use their words to place blame, create shame, or complain.

As ridiculous as it seems that someone would ignore an elderly, disabled person's benefit from courtesy at a door, it is just as ridiculous to feign colorblindness. It is our choice to see or not see others that lead to disconnects in relationships. Nobody wants to be invisible.

We each get to choose how and when we relate to others. If we desire to build and establish relationships in our respective communities, companies, on our jobs or in our places of worship, we are capable of learning how to see people as they see themselves and have to take the initiative to learn their perspective as much as possible. When we see and acknowledge cultural realities that affect day-to-day life, we empower ourselves and others to live with authenticity, creativity, collaboration, and enriching engagement with each other.

Just as there are certain behaviors that put Mr. Will at even greater risk because of his life situation, there are behaviors that can be intentional and/or ignorant that can put the lives of people of color at risk, or simply make their lives harder and the lives of everybody else less inclusive of them. As we prepare to talk through the five cultural blinders we've identified, we believe you will learn how to spot and eliminate those behaviors in your various communities and organizations.

We don't recommend approaching color and race with the golden rule, "Do unto others as YOU would have others do unto you." Instead, we ask you to consider application of the platinum rule[vi] when engaging with cultural counterparts where we, "Treat others as THEY would have you do unto them." We can't rewrite history nor should we try; however, we can be more intentional in how we value, honor, and attribute dignity and respect to those we encounter daily.

One example of this is dining with international students. Each year, universities, like the University of Arkansas, put out a request for local families to host international students for holiday dinners. When we accept the invitation

---

vi   Alessandra, T., The Platinum Rule (n.d.). Retrieved from http://www.alessandra. com/abouttony/aboutpr.asp.

to invite students into our homes, we could prepare OUR favorite meal to "do unto others as I would have them do unto me." I (Angela) would love to go to someone's home and have a delicious pork roast with carrots and mashed potatoes and Black beans with bacon and bacon grease in the seasoning. Yummmm! That is one of my favorite meals, so why wouldn't I share that meal with students for a holiday celebration? Or another American holiday favorite, ham?

If we are thinking of "Do unto others as THEY would have us do unto them," we consider the fact that Muslim international students do not eat pork. So, the best chance of honoring them and building relationships with them is to "see culture" and to refrain from cooking pork at those meals. Seeing color is akin to seeing culture. It is a matter of being mindful, knowing that everything in our diverse worlds is not the same. We are not all the same under the skin. We can see color and culture and honor one another as we have been born into the world and as our cultures and experiences have formed us.

Consider also a blank canvas without color - it fails to reveal any concept, image or shape until there is interaction between the artist, the brush, the paint colors, and the canvas to reveal the artist's idea and emotion. The viewer who beholds the work also experiences the work through their own perception and experiences. The viewer will wonder and think about the image unless they have been taught to dismiss or are ignorant of the creativity or color within the painted canvas. In other words, the purpose of a blank canvas goes unfulfilled until it is met with communication and creativity by the artist from her or his imagination, and its most important attributes – color and contrast. Relationships may feel like this at the beginning – there is ignorance of creativity, uncertainty of what will unfold, and it will take time to yield the attributes of greatest importance in the journey. Without finishing the work, no one else could see what had the potential to manifest.

When we choose to engage with cultural groups who are different from our own, we begin to form relationships like that of the artist, brush, and color with life's canvas. We then can modify or inform our perception which will, in turn, change our reality, enabling us to use our power of notice and visibility. Thus, when we choose to take notice, it is only then that we come to appreciate the value and purpose of color!

---

*"We all should know that diversity makes for a rich tapestry, and we must understand that all the threads of the tapestry are equal in value no matter what their color."*

---

*~Maya Angelou*

# 2

# DEFINING COLOR

Why does color exist? Color serves to allow expression of personality or meaning through light that reflects the beauty that is in the world in which we live. Look at the colors we used for this book – the colors are multifaceted, bold, bright, and brilliant.

Color does not exist to bring separation or division; rather, color exists to bring light, interest, emotion, and perspective. Color serves as a connector - a compliment to its contrast. It helps us to express our personality and experiences while it serves as a framework of expression for our respective worlds. It is a backdrop by which we can infuse values and culture.

In the physical world, color is a perception based on the refraction of light rays that enter into our eyes. There are instances where color is not perceivable. When this occurs, it is because some peoples' physical eyes literally don't fully perceive color. We call this person colorblind. They perceive brown as blue or blue as green and they perceive color differently or not at all as compared to most of us. A person's options may be limited by physical color blindness which is an ability challenge that was not chosen. Some careers such as flying an airplane are not an option for the physically colorblind person. Cultural colorblindness is a chosen disability that creates limitation and may cause one to do harm to others.

Similarly, in the world in which we live with our racialized histories, color is both a perceptual and a cultural identity issue. The identity of who a person is may not be consistent with our perception of them. We may not see key facts regarding who they are as a human being if we chose to ignore important aspects of their experiences and culture. Seeing color provides clues into the different experiences, ideas, and struggles from our own. If we operate by the dismissive illusion that we are all the same versus the reality that we have different experiences and preferences based on our cultural realities, we don't really "see" each other.

In the last few years, we've both encountered conversations where we have heard our white or Caucasian friends and family say, "I don't see color." We recognize their attempt to express acceptance and similarity by saying "I don't see color" but this actually does more harm than good. Not seeing color makes most people of color feel as if they are invisible or not seen for who they are as human beings contributing and sharing their gifts and talents with the world. Instead, there is a sudden statement that begins to dismiss and negate the struggles that non-whites face simply because of the color of their skin. It also presumes that being white is the "normal" or the "right way to be" when anyone pretends not to see color and subsequently not recognize the experiences that go with having more melanin in a historically racist culture.

These embedded biases are inherent in our communication as we have historical, political, and socioeconomic consequences that have influenced the reality of our current environment. The realities of racism persist, often giving preference and legitimizing the ideas, wants, needs and concerns of white people over the needs, experiences, and even lives of people of color.

This book serves to address five blinders that we have in a society where we state that we don't see color and the impact it has on historically marginalized groups in the United States.

# 3

## BLINDER 1: ANXIETY and UNCERTAINTY

Anxiety and Uncertainty Management (AUM) research[vii] indicates that people are quite often anxious and uncertain about how to behave in situations when they meet a new person of any ethnicity or gender. Anxiety is an emotional process (having feelings of fear, nervousness, etc.). Uncertainty is a thinking process (not being certain how to behave appropriately given the unknowns about the person). This phenomena is heightened in interracial/cultural encounters when one or both of the people lacks experience (practice) interacting with members of ethnic groups outside of their own and when either person perceives the other person to be of a different ethnic group both anxiety and uncertainty are escalated. This is out of concern that the interaction goes well. People want to make positive impressions and most people want to treat others well.

---

vii  Gudykunst, W (2005). An anxiety/uncertainty management (AUM) Theory of effective communication: Making the mesh of the net finer. In W.B. Gudykunst (Ed.). Theorizing about intercultural communication (pp. 281-322). Thousand Oaks, CA: Sage.

Imagine the anxiety (nervousness) and uncertainty (overthinking) experienced before and during your first date, dance, or other social event without your parents. This is the same kind of anxiety and uncertainty produced when we have cross cultural and interracial encounters with people whom we are not yet familiar.

Sometimes these first encounters fail because we make mistakes that are not understood by the other person. Often our anxiety or embarrassment from "mistakes" becomes so high that we simply do not try again. We may become even more confused about why our attempts at communicating and connecting failed. The result is often avoidance, or even worse, shame and blame.

Since we all tend to evaluate ourselves based on our intention, not necessarily the outcomes or impact of our failure, it is likely that we may shift from being anxious and confused to blaming the other person for the failure of communication efforts. We can have a self-serving bias that favors us and shifts responsibility to the other person.

The blame-shame game: We know that blame produces shame, hiding, and fear, which results in retreat. So, what is the result? Instead of visibility and vulnerability, we get self-segregation, secrets, silos, and a lack of trust. Trust is necessary to take the risks to build stable, mutual, and satisfying relationships of any kind in both personal and professional contexts.

When we retreat and segregate ourselves, we create more division which fosters continued feelings of isolation and breeds infidelity in our communication with members of the "other" group. The lack of communication then creates an opportunity for real or perceived fear of being mistreated or misunderstood.

Whether real or perceived, fear and mistrust limit our ability to build healthy relationships. Fear in the race and culture context tends to be based on three things:

1. Fear of looking bad to others
2. Fear of failing/hurting others
3. Fear of being hurt by others (emotional, reputation, etc.)

Fear of looking bad to others occurs when an individual is part of a community that has accepted norms and behaviors that get challenged when (s)he steps outside of the community by different norms and behaviors. The perception is that assimilation into the new community is required in order for one to FIT into the environment versus the one choosing to stick to the communication patterns of their dominant culture. This is where a skill referred to as code switching occurs. People of Color code switch more often because the predominantly white environment requires it of them to be perceived more successfully. This is a communication competence that most people of color possess, and many white people do not.

Using language that is outside of the dominant culture of a community can be one way to save face when afraid. For example instead of saying "Yahweh" or "Yahshua" because that is the Hebrew name for God (Yahweh) and Jesus (Yahshua), one might say God and Jesus because it is easier and more accepted than to face the fear of having to explain your position or beliefs as they are outside the majority accepted norms and behavioral expectation.

Next, fear of failing or hurting others can cause anxiety. Making mistakes can not only be embarrassing, but they can be hurtful. The Anxiety and Uncertainty Management (AUM) theory discussed previously covers the anxiety (or feeling of fear) because an interaction with a person is important. Wanting the interaction to go well is partially based in the concern for the well-being of the other. This kind of fear is actually helpful in motivating us to do our best to learn to understand and communicate according to the needs and preferences of those we work and live around in order to eliminate misunderstandings and achieve as much mutual satisfaction as possible. Adapting to the needs or preferences of cultural groups is called cultural competence.

Fear of being hurt by others often means being diminished or invisible to others. If someone says "I Am Beautiful" and the response is "Aren't we all," we have created the idea that the unique beauty of the one individual making the statement is discounted and irrelevant as compared to the collective. The effort to be inclusive by saying "aren't we all" hurts the individual whose personal history may be filled with many saying (s)he was not beautiful. Now the experience that should have been empowering and uplifting because it was her first time releasing these words over herself is diminished because of someone's awkward attempt to include everyone.

The awkward attempt toward inclusion implies that there is a "sense of absolutes" for every situation. When a mistake is made concerning color or racial categorization, the experiences, real or perceived, inform future engagement. Individuals shift to self-preservation over preservation of the relationship causing discomfort and damaging impact to communication and creativity.

If communication for connection is not of importance to personal ego or identity, it doesn't create much consequence when failure presents itself. Imagine attempting to make a soufflé and it tanks, no one will see the result of the failure except those who share the space. Those who are close understand the failure in the context of the attempt to try a new dish as a creative cook and not a chef.

However, in the context where an individual is on social media and wants to engage or learn in an intellectual conversation, any logic that is challenged beyond comprehension may create a feeling of incompetence which leads to a retreat from the discussion (partially because of the public aspect of social media, and public failure). This retreat persists if the replies are shameful, blaming or attacking personal character. The result is self-segregation to protect the ego/identity. This plays out not only in interpersonal communication but also in dyadic (one on one) and group relationships.

Consider an American Black female in a corporate environment who asks leaders questions to gain clarity on changes in the organization, process, or structure. When she asks questions, she is often perceived as being (and then told that she is) intimidating. Because she is perceived as "intimidating" her questions are taken as challenges rather than as intended, to exercise her natural inclination to ask clarifying questions when she does not fully comprehend. When she asks questions to get an understanding of what makes her "intimidating" no one is able or willing to provide examples or explanations.

Career advances (for this same American Black Female) or promotions aren't necessarily seen as a result of competence for her skill but rather devalued as "Affirmative Action" which she did not merit. A perception is created and perpetuated by people who perceive her through their own biases, anxieties, and uncertainties. Feedback resulting from these perceptions is that she (the Black Female) "needs to work on relationship management as a competency" because the ego of positional leaders is challenged when she asks questions.

The power to perceive, interpret, and apply one's own ego/identity and biases to her gives them organizational and personal power to perpetuate the idea that she is "an angry Black woman" rather than identify and take responsibility for their own anxiety, uncertainty, and lack of understanding on how to communicate clearly without feeling challenged by questions.

This happens frequently in organizations all over the United States. The Black (or brown) woman (or man) simply attempts to clarify concerns or questions as a member of the team, as is their job to do. Instead of asserting ego or power, leaders have the opportunity to choose to communicate concerns and questions. Their concerns or questions are often mistaken to be challenges or implicitly believed to be the person of color not "knowing their place" even though their "place" legally and in their job or positional role IS to ask those questions. The implicit (unstated) rules of the organization or the other employees in question may be that "you don't challenge me."

The result of encounters such as this is fear for the Black female professional to move forward toward collaboration and connectivity through communication when people in the position of power have the authority to define her communication (and character) of questioning and to label it as something malicious. They stifle the very inclination to lead with influence and thought leadership she was hired to bring to the organization.

The failure to understand and to be understood triggers the blame game, creates personal shame, and self-segregation by both parties. Self-segregation is avoidance. Failure may damage self-esteem or reputation.

Why care about reputation? Our reputation is connected to our identities, our character, and how we see ourselves and treat others. However, reputation is also a reflection of our ego and in a materialistic society where what we wear, say, and do is always on display, the name we build for ourselves sometimes creates a façade that yields a greater sense of fear beyond what might exist in a world that had less access to our personal media. This perpetuates our need to protect our image by creating an environment that forces us to self-segregate when we feel invisible or incompetent on any topic, but especially those topics that challenge or expose our fears or lack of competence such as color and/or race.

# 4

## BLINDER 2:
## POWER MISUSED

Power is often treated as a "dirty word" in the U.S. American vocabulary. Although most people have some type of power, we don't like to admit it, because we do not understand it. Power is neutral, not good, or bad. Power is a thing that exists in the universe, in nature, in humans. Power is inherent in our personalities; we all hold different types of power. Mothers often hold a special power to comfort. Children hold a special power to make us smile and soften our hearts. Politicians have special powers to make laws, or to change laws. Tellers have special powers to access our bank accounts. Whether power is good or bad depends upon the way in which we use it.

There are four types of power that affect our ability to see race or color accurately: social, legitimate/positional, personal, and economic. In Blinder One we talked about positional/legitimate power a little bit and we will expand on that more here.

Americans tend to use power liberally, despite an unspoken taboo to acknowledge the power available. When we talk about power, who immediately comes to mind? Power may be inherent in our nationality, race, gender, economic or financial position. Power gives us the ability to influence not only our own circumstances but also social or political outcomes. Power that we did not earn or accumulate through our own work is known in the academic literature as "privilege." All privilege is not equivalent. For instance, being born into a wealthy family, being born male, being born American, and having a college education paid for give advantages that others do not have throughout the world.

Privilege is unearned power. Because a person does not feel privileged doesn't mean that they aren't privileged. Our aim is to help you recognize that privilege has layers. Here's an example: obtaining a college education is a benefit. If someone obtains a college education that was paid for by someone else that is a form of privilege. If it was given to an individual by inheritance or favor of any kind, that is considered privilege. Privilege differs for the one whose education was paid for by someone else--an unearned benefit--as opposed to the person who received grants or loans or work jobs while going through school. Both received an education – one was privileged, and one was earned. A person who has received the benefit of unearned power has an advantage over those who have not received the same benefit albeit through knowledge or wealth transfer. For instance, 2nd or 3rd generation students or entrepreneurs have not only shared knowledge with those who came before them but also ready access to expert help. This term "privilege" is often misunderstood as an accusation of wrongdoing rather than a statistically validated fact of advantage.

## Social power

Social power is often used to dismiss the experiences of people of color and silence their voices. This has occurred when a white person makes a claim of having it "just as bad" because they were poor growing up. This is known as a false equivalency. In other words, we may claim that one person's poverty experience is no better or worse than our own personal poverty experience. This is dismissive and often untrue.

For example: A poor white person is not the same as a poor person of color. The poor white person has a better chance of majority blending in and getting assistance than the poor person of color. The poor white person could change their attire, leave her neighborhood and be perceived as acceptable, trustworthy, and a "good fit" for a job applied for, or even to be perceived as wealthy. On the other hand, this is more difficult for the American Black or African American person with a similar background who could go buy the same nice clothes and step outside their neighborhood. The data on pay gap alone indicates that a Black woman may not be accepted or perceived as well as the socioeconomically-similar white woman. The key difference is race. White skin has a social power.

In this example, and often in American organizations from the boardroom to the baptistry. A white person has more social power because one is perceived consistently as more qualified, and more "innocent" than the other regardless of similar backgrounds, educational qualifications, job experience, public service, or personal histories.

Social power can also be used to help promote fairness, equality, diversity, and inclusivity in one's community and all the organizations to which one belongs. Organizational communication research and systems theory conclude that it takes both insiders and outsiders to change organizations and systems. Predominantly white organizations may be more likely to initially listen to insider (white) voices, but knowing what needs to change to make people of color feel more welcome requires listening to people of color (who may be outsiders to the organization or its leadership teams).

## Legitimate or positional power

Legitimate or positional power is defined as the ability to influence fellow members of a group which is usually dependent on status within the group and one's recognized right to require and demand compliance of others[viii].

---

viii  M.S., P. (2015, July 13). What is LEGITIMATE POWER? definition of LEGITIMATE POWER (Psychology Dictionary). Retrieved from https://psychologydictionary.org/legitimate-power

Legitimate power is the power of the supervisor to reward and punish.

In a previous example, we see the (legitimate) power to include remarks in the annual review of the Black woman stating that she "needs to work on the competency of relationship development" based on the implicit bias of the leader, and anxiety when she asks questions. The supervisor's legitimate power in this case was used to do harm to her career with such perceptions and comments, and failure to use one's legitimate power ethically.

Legitimate/Positional power can also be used to mentor, promote, and advocate for people one prefers. It is frequently done for those who get promoted to top levels. Their names are mentioned by people with positional power over lunch, on the golf course, they may even be invited to join and be included by people with positional power, which gives them access that others do not receive. Research indicates that casual access to people in positional power outside of organizational roles (such as going to dinner together, playing golf, or going to the same place of worship) is partially responsible for the "glass ceiling" effect and the lack of inclusion at the top levels of industry, government, and society. If those who we have social access to are those who have the power to hire, promote, and recommend us then we have more opportunity.

## Personal power

Personal power is simply a person's personal characteristics that make others likely to listen to and follow them. The businessdictionary.com definition of personal power states[ix] that it is "influence over others, the source of which resides in the person instead of being vested by the position he or she holds."

There are people with "personal power" throughout history who possessed an ability to influence people to do things we may find unthinkable in our modern context. It is important to note that some who we may now consider "unrighteous leaders" did so during a time where the "Great Man theory" persisted in people's assumptions of the traits a leader worth following and pledging allegiance to should possess. The name suggests the first qualification of the time (and perhaps still) was being male. Some other traits have been, ability to speak well and with authoritative certainty to influence many, ability to use personal power combined with legitimate power to negotiate the "systems" within which they operated, ability to incite fear in people to trigger or maintain inhumane behaviors, laws, and policies.

Personal power can also be used to lead through times of trouble. Many great leaders such as Dr. Martin Luther King Jr. and Sojourner Truth used personal attributes,

---

ix    What is personal power? definition and meaning. (n.d.). Retrieved from http://www.businessdictionary.com/definition/personal-power.html

talents, experiences, and their ability to persuade people to listen, and reconsider. People who use personal power often do not have assigned positions of legitimate power, however their message and character are so compelling that they have great influence.

## Economic power

Economic power is the financial power of individuals and groups to control the economy, media, business, elections/candidate financing (which essentially becomes the power to buy policies and lawmakers that favor one group and may ignore or even harm other groups through personal access and lobbying).

If we look at the demographics of who holds economic power in the United States of America and any other country in the world, we can see who holds the power to control every system in that country. Countries with the most economic power (such as the United States) hold much power to control world affairs, policies, and other countries through both punitive and reward measures.

Economic power applies the same on an individual level as it does on the macro level of nations and countries. Individuals who have more economic power have more influence on their own environments and the environments of others. They have more influence on their community organizations, churches, and even workplaces. Combined with positional/legitimate power, economic power gives people not only the "right" to make certain decisions about the abilities and intentions and promotions of others, but also puts people with economic resources in position to be considered or "top of mind" for their own advancement as well.

Think back about our social power example of golfing. Not only does golfing with the boss or the guys give someone access to the boss in a social context, but it is also shown to make that person more known on a personal level, more on the mind of the decision makers who he has personal relationships with outside of work. Not only is this a privilege that is largely reserved for males (because of social/religious beliefs regarding segregated socialization between males and females outside of work such as the "Billy Graham Rule").

Golf is expensive. To be able to golf with the boss, one not only must own certain expensive equipment, but also have had long term access to expensive golf clubs, lessons, golf rounds in order to play well enough to be invited to play with the boss. Economic power makes it possible to gain even more economic power.

We are not saying that it is bad to play golf with the boss. What we are saying is that to no fault of their own, some people are excluded from the opportunities and relationships this fosters because they have been both systematically and intentionally excluded by both laws, policies, economics, and personal racism from having similar opportunities.

Those individuals and organizations who have benefited from both privilege (unearned benefits - college paid for by parents, being born male, being white, etc.) and hard work must in good conscience consider how we might assist others who have put in the hard work, but not had the benefit of privilege (a few unearned lucky breaks).

# 5

# BLINDER 3:
# EGOcentrism

Every human has an ego and it's not all bad. Ego is part of our personal identity; however, one's ego can cause them to behave badly when we let it hinder our ability to exercise care or concern beyond ourselves, our family, or our own cultural group.

Our ego is our sense of self. This includes our identity as a member of an ethnic and/or cultural group. Even people who say they "don't see color" or who do not actively think about their ancestors still have an identity, a self-developed thought about how they think of themselves. Part of this perceived self involves our experiences as members of different groups. For instance, part of our identity/ego is affected by our Nationality and how we feel about that Nationality. Most Americans are happy they are Americans, although they may not understand how much "privilege" they have because of being born an American with all the rights Americans have that may not be afforded to citizens of other countries. Being an American or an immigrant, or a female may be part of your identity. How you feel about those parts of yourself and your life is part of your Ego.

Power research indicates that people who have high levels of power, (legitimate/positional and economic) are at risk to think more highly of themselves than others think of them according to the feedback of others who work for and around them. They also tend to believe their decisions are sounder than others believe (and that their track record proves). People with high levels of power also think of themselves as fairer than others think they are. This is known as self-serving-bias. When ego gets in the way, we may tend to see ourselves and our performance as better than it is. We may also believe that others feel more positively and think more highly about us than they do.

Egocentrism is an inflated sense of self, a self-centered view of the world, and causes us to see ourselves and people who we perceive to be like ourselves in less than factual or honest ways. It also causes us to do harm to people we see as "different" or as "other" than ourselves or our group. This is known as ingroup/outgroup thinking. Being a member of the dominant population in any nation or community can create a collective and individual egocentrism that is unaware or even intentionally harms people from less dominant populations.

## In-group / Out-group thinking
## (racial egocentrism)

Our in-group is the people we see as similar to ourselves; the out-group is anyone who we see as dissimilar and not "our people." Every person has an "in-group" and an "out-group." Our goal in discussing this Ingroup/Outgroup phenomena is to help readers become more aware of our own thinking and who we are likely to see as "suspicious" or even less deserving of dignity because they come from different places in life, have different communication codes/styles, have cultural preferences that are different than our own and may even look or dress differently than ourselves.

Ingroup/Outgroup research indicates that humans tend to be socialized by groups (family, community, faith, etc.) that we perceive as "our people" or NOT "our people." We tend to react upon the first cues of who is "my people" based upon visual information of physical likeness. Ethnic/racial differences are impossible to "not see." If we are not aware of this human tendency we will subconsciously perceive, feel, and behave in ways that either humanize or dehumanize people from ethnic groups outside of our own.

## Ingroup Members

Ingroup members are people whose welfare we ARE concerned about and for whom we do not demand equitable returns in order to collaborate or assist[x].

---

x     Gudykunst, W., & Kim, Y. (1997). *Communicating with strangers: An integrated approach to intercultural communication.* (3 ed.). Boston: McGraw-Hill.

Ingroup members are individuals or groups of people who we associate as *similar* to ourselves based on physical, cultural, linguistic similarity or geographic proximity.

Ingroup members get our assistance or collaboration without the expectation of equitable returns although there may be an expectation of being seen favorably and receiving favors or consideration in future unknown situations. We give ingroup members assistance with job searches and recommendations of many types, connecting them to other ingroup members who may help, roadside assistance, general politeness even with ingroup member strangers in public places.

Separation from in-group members brings discomfort or even pain.

## Outgroup Members

Outgroup members are people or groups whose welfare we are NOT concerned about and from whom we demand equitable returns in order to collaborate or assist. Outgroup members are individuals or groups of people who we associate as DIS*similar* to ourselves based on physical, cultural, linguistic similarity or geographic proximity.

Pejorative, demeaning terms about outgroup members are often viewed as socially—and even professionally—excusable. Dehumanization is a key component of outgroup treatment. It allows us to behave and communicate in ways that would be inappropriate and even immoral towards people we know and care about or even strangers who would be perceived as in-group members.

Outgroup members are people who we are less likely to render our assistance if needed, if we see an outgroup member's car disabled on the side of the road, or if they are being racially or sexually harassed in public by ingroup members we are more likely to look away.

When outgroup members are not present, we feel no discomfort or pain, as a matter of fact, those who have implicit biases are likely to feel discomfort and high levels of anxiety when outgroup members are present[xi].

One study showed that European Americans who had racially biased attitudes performed lower on simple cognitive tests immediately after interacting with African Americans than they performed on the same tests before the interactions. So interaction with outgroup members even puts additional stress on brain function for people who have subconscious and conscious racial bias, the more biased a person is, the more taxed their brain is when interacting outside of their own ethnic group[xii].

---

xi    Gudykunst, W., & Kim, Y. (1997). Communicating with strangers: An integrated approach to *intercultural communication*. (3 ed.). Boston: McGraw-Hill.

xii   Cook, G. 2003, Richeson et al, 2003, Trawalter, et al., 2009 as cited in Orbe & Harris.

## Angela's German Accent Story

When I (Angela) was a pre-teen I moved from Berlin, Germany to Fayetteville, North Carolina. I had no memory of living in the United States. My early childhood and school days were spent mostly in Europe, Italy, and Germany to be specific. My first memories are of the Italian neighbors crowding the whole family of eight onto their balcony to see the little American girls with blue eyes. They liked to touch us, they were affectionate, they spoke Italian, and from an early age I came to understand that there were different languages and customs and ways of dressing, thinking, and looking everywhere I went. This was my "normal."

I returned "home" to the American deep South with a German accent. My German accent and cultural mannerisms made me stick out like a sore thumb. I remember being picked on and even beat up on more than one occasion because people thought I was speaking German and they couldn't understand me. One day, my ponytail was cut off on the school bus. As a result, my once long locks ended up being reshaped into a "pixie" cut, resembling the cut of a young boy. I hadn't hit puberty quite yet, so I looked like a boy, and had a German accent. I was made fun of because of the accent, because of "looking like a boy," because of being different, even by the other military kids in our neighborhood who had not lived overseas.

There was also the time that for about a month when a boy in high school who was a few grades older (and at least a foot taller) chased me down every day after I got off the school bus. I raced to my house, but he always caught me before I got to the door, knocked me down and proceeded to kick me until he was bored. I was never sure if it was because I was white, because I was a girl, or because of my still thick German accent. What I was sure of is that I was an "outsider" and thus an easy target. These are examples of outgroup treatment.

## What Angela learned from being an outsider

Outgroup members have a keen awareness of the cultural ideas and expectations of ingroup members because those ways seem strange to the outsider, newcomer, or "stranger." Newcomers to organizations are more alert to organizational cultures (like schools, churches, businesses) than old-timers in them are because the culture has become "normal" to those who've stayed awhile.

One of my first realizations, when I came to live in the United States, was that "Americans are mean." I much preferred my friends at school back in Germany. I much preferred the people in church fellowships (held in metal military buildings) in Germany. The people in America were mean, even the church people. Americans said mean words I had never heard before about anyone who didn't look like or agree with them, especially Black people. This seemed very wrong to me, and I couldn't find where this was what was in alignment with the teachings of Jesus.

I first heard the "N" word was at a church full of white people (except for one soldier from the nearby military base who was of Mexican descent), which seemed strange in the first place. I knew there were brown and Black people in North Carolina because there were Black kids in my school, and there were people from different countries because of the military base. I saw people of different ethnicities and nationalities at school, on the bus, and in the neighborhood. Yet, only white people attended the church our father drove us 45 minutes from home to attend three times a week.

I learned that people were mean. I learned that some people were loved and treated well, and others were not. I also learned that the church could be as mean a place as the school bus and that white people, especially men, were the only really important people in this strange "new world." I learned that I was not one of the important people. I was an "outsider" wherever I went, always the one with an accent, the newcomer, or "just a white girl" as I would later be labeled when I married across the color/ culture line.

Of course, I didn't understand the complexities or the histories of trauma our ancestors had inflicted, and then continued to blame the victims. It was all very confusing, and especially in the light of the Bible stories I'd heard and read. Of course, the older and more able to think for myself I became, the stronger my sense of disconnect became between what we were taught in Sunday School, and how we justified treating "outsiders" on the school bus, or worse yet, in their absence. Because of my own experiences, I learned to pay attention to "outsiders" and to try to be a friend to "strangers." It made me feel comforted for my own outsider-ness, but I felt that, somehow, being kind also made a place of safety and comfort for a few other people as well ... if only for brief moments.

## The Power of Language

What we say and how we say words matters. When we speak, our choice of words enables the listener to discern and/or decide how to interpret the intent and meaning. As we know, efforts to communicate can be correctly, incorrectly, or partially heard, interpreted, read, or perceived.

When we add race or color to the conversation, it further compounds the communication challenge. Language informs how we engage and relate to others within and outside of our groups. In most cases, language choice also reflects the unconscious belief systems (about others) that are inherent within each of us.

An old proverb we heard growing up says, "for out of the abundance of the heart the mouth speaks." We believe this principle because there is a relationship between the conscious mind and the subconscious. Our cognitions (thinking in the mind) are reflections of our affections (feelings and beliefs of the subconscious mind). Our affect (emotional demonstration) forms our cognition (thoughts) which are reflected in our verbalizations. In other words, feelings + thoughts = communication (verbal and non-verbal). Our language choice (even "Freudian slips") allow us to codify what we believe to be reality and truth by putting thoughts and feelings into words. Neuroscience research supports this idea and can offer greater insight.

Language is used to create and maintain real or perceived power or to establish dominance. In relationships where abuse is present, the individual in power often demeans or belittles the abused by using words to establish and deepen their position.

Consider a child who grows up in an environment where racist language is used as part of daily conversation. When he or she goes to college away from home, he or she may continue use of the same language and find it met unfavorably if they are outside of their ingroup environment.

When we are unaware of our bias - or blinders - we tend to continue to engage in behaviors that could impact our opportunity to invest in getting to know members of the outgroup. To get a greater awareness of our biases, particularly regarding race, color, or gender, we recommend participating in the Harvard University research known as Project Implicit. This project began in 1998 and contains a series of Implicit Association Tests that can help bring awareness to the unconscious biases you may hold.

In an April 2017 article, Lisa Alexander shared some insights on the results of millennials who took Harvard's Bias Test[xiii]. Alexander stated that the results of the individuals who opted to participate, were able to find their bias in their personal history and that it was helpful to do this test BEFORE engaging in any group environment where the topic of conversation would be gender, appearance, race or color related[xiv].

xiii  Alexander, L., & Alexander, L. (2017, April 10). These Millennials Took Harvard's Bias Test–Here's What They Learned. Retrieved from https://www.fastcompany.com/40404485/these-millennials-took-harvards-bias-test-heres-what-they-learned.

xiv  Project Implicit. (2011). Implicit Association Test. Retrieved from https://implicit.harvard.edu/implicit/takeatest.html.

## LaTonya in the Philippines

Being the child of a member of the armed forces affords some unique experiences. For LaTonya, this included a stint in the Philippines during school age. My classes were full of individuals from many nations and as a result, created opportunities to learn about other cultures and heritage beyond my own. I learned patience and a way to communicate and build relationships that transcended language barriers.

Upon return to the United States in the late '80s I moved to Mississippi and then to Nebraska and found myself in environments where I was among the African American population and became very aware of my own skin color. It wasn't until graduate school during an encounter with a faculty member that I recognized the impact that my stint in the Philippines had on my ability to communicate and relate to individuals in groups outside of my own.

During an advising discussion, the faculty member asked a question about where I was from. Perplexed, I answered, "Mississippi," to which he replied, "No." Now intrigued, I asked for clarity. The faculty member said, "You're not from around here, where are you *from*?" This time, I responded with "I was a military brat, so I've lived in different places." "Where?" asked the faculty member. I responded, "Texas, Mississippi, Philippines, Nebraska." This time the faculty replied, "That's it. That's the difference. You're not *from* here."

Why is this relevant to our discussion? The faculty member was from Africa and often had students complain about the difficulty in relating to him or understanding what he was saying when he taught. I, LaTonya, never seemed to have this issue, and when there was a barrier, I knew how to press in to get clarity. That experience as a child provided me with the framework to remove blinders and "seek first to understand" (Covey[xv]) rather than be understood when in conversation with a member of the "other" or "outside" group than my own. It was LaTonya's choice of words and her non-verbal behavior that led to this discussion with her faculty member which highlighted a difference in her of which she was unaware.

Being perceived as an "outsider" is a constant state of being asked or treated as if "You're not from around here, are you?" or worse yet, "You don't belong here." One does not have to know "everything" about outgroup members in order to relate and communicate well, one simply needs to be mindful that there are multiple ways of being and doing things that are "right" and sometimes more effective than the "ways" we learned in our original cultural groups and families.

In LaTonya's example with her advisor, her language and thoughtfulness, also known as mindfulness, were used to foster a relationship versus hinder it. Language does not have to be what divides us regarding race or color. It can

---

xv  Covey, S. (2004). Seven Habits of Highly Effective People. Free Press.

be what unifies us if we learn to think, learn, and listen to each other, especially people who we may first perceive as "not from around here."

## Problems with the way we talk

Debate is valuable for discourse to decide public policy, but it is not really effective for building interpersonal relationships. Debate often becomes a power struggle rather than a problem-solving conversation between two people or two people groups. Debate is an American tradition, but it has its limitations.

It is not effective in interracial encounters to debate. This context is best for listening to each other instead of "debating" one another's experiences. When a person of color shares experiences of oppressive treatment, they are often met with debate as to whether they perceived it correctly, what they should have done differently, and even why it was their fault. Communicating in this way does not build understanding or relationships. Just imagine if you did this when your significant other tells you they had a rough day. Your relationship would be tense, and perhaps not last very long, or there would be constant discontent. This is our current American situation due to our lack of listening to each other.

When people share vulnerable information about what hurts, what we need to do is to empathetically listen to each other, and engage in healthy dialogue, which can be uncomfortable, but should not be emotionally or physically unsafe. When we can listen and extend empathy, we will build trusting friendships. This is missing between white and Black America— just being kind humans who share and listen to each other on the individual and the community levels.

The plaque on the statue of liberty says, "Give me your tired, your poor, your huddled masses yearning to be free, The wretched refuse of your teeming shore, send these, the homeless, tempest-lost to me. I lift my lamp beside the golden door"[xvi].

Our Declaration of Independence states, "All men are created equal." The historical evidence makes clear that the assumption and cultural context for this statement was understood to be, "All white, free, land-owning men are created equal." It's time as a society that we delete the assumptions of anybody being "disqualified" because of race or gender. It's time we fulfill the promise our forefathers made but never intended for us "all." As Dr. King stated, it is a check that has been marked "insufficient funds."

Do we really want to be egocentric and ethnocentric, and continue as a society focused on me and my people only? Let us learn to regard everybody instead of just a few who we recognize as our "ingroup" members. Color

---

xvi Lazarus, E. (1883). The New Colossus.

exists--and rather than saying, "I don't see color," we could choose to say, "I see you, too. I want to see you more clearly, and want to get to know your history, too."

# 6

**BLINDER 4:
IGNORANCE**

We are ignorant of the devices that keep us divided. Some of that ignorance can be attributed to the education we received regarding race or color in America and how it was presented. A 2018 article highlighted changes that Texas schools were just making to be implemented in 2019 textbooks regarding slavery[xvii]. Texas and many other schools in America have taught that the Civil War was a war primarily about the States Rights, completely denying at times that it had anything to do with slavery. Recently we received news of an assignment a Texas teacher gave, asking students to list the "positive" and "negative" aspects of slavery[xviii]. The public news stories regarding these situations only highlight what has been taking place all along to misinform and miseducate us all on the history of race in America. African American history has been

---

xvii  Monroe, B. (2011, May 25). How Texas' School Board Tried to Pretend Slavery Never Happened and Why Your Kid's School May Be Next. Retrieved from https://www.huffingtonpost.com/bryan-monroe/how-texas-school-board-tr_b_586633.html.

xviii Ventura, C. (2018, April 21). Texas school apologizes for asking students to list 'positive aspects' of slavery. Retrieved from https://www.usatoday.com/story/news/nation/2018/04/21/school-slavery-homework-assignment-texas/538770002/

63

taught in predominantly Black communities and schools by Black teachers and parents and predominantly Black churches. Their oral traditions are what kept the history and experiences of their ancestors active. What resulted from this was a clear delineation of historical accounts taught in schools today as students matriculate and assimilate into more predominant cultural environments. As a result, we don't have a full historical picture from one community to the other unless we're connecting and sharing information across community and cultural boundaries.

Historically, school districts have been run by local school boards. Districts in the south have been predominantly white. Thus, in collaboration and pacts with the Daughters of the Confederacy, much of history has been intentionally left out of the curriculum, including the centrality of slavery as the reason for the Civil War. This history has been preserved in oral traditions of the African American community and in local news accounts glorifying incidents such as lynching.

When we discussed fear/anxiety, we asked the question, "What are we afraid of?" We're afraid of fear itself. We're anxious about going into conversations, situations, and relationships where we don't know what to expect and we're concerned about making errors.

## The Role of Privilege

The term "privilege" is tough, and it feels like an accusation of doing intentional harm. That is why it can be triggering for many people. If you will, could you take a deep breath right here with us? Breathe ...breathe . . . Now, can we talk? What is privilege, who has it, and how does privilege blind us? Let's breathe again as we engage this discussion ... Breathe ... breathe .

What is privilege? Having privilege does not mean that your life has been easy or even that you have done something wrong. It means your predecessors established a system that favors you more than others. We can think of privilege as being favored, getting a head start, and being (more) insulated. The examples below are designed to provide clarity.

A man can grow up poor, have no inheritance or money to start with, and still have an advantage over a woman from comparable conditions when applying for a job they are both similarly qualified for. If those doing the hiring are more "comfortable" working with men, or have a bias against women or their abilities, the man will get the job simply because he's a qualified man. This is known as male privilege. Male privilege is common in historically paternalistic cultures. The United States is a historically paternalistic culture. Evidence of this is that women were not granted the right to vote, own their own property, have custody of their children, or get a divorce until the suffrage movement in the 1920's.

Privilege is having unearned favor or the benefit of the doubt in the culture simply because of the conditions and/ or package to which one was born. Unearned meaning a person did not "earn" this condition, they were simply born into it. There are many layers of privilege, and few people have them all; however, the more layers a person has, the more "insulated" and protected that person is from everyday difficulties such as the consequences of a traffic violation.

Who has privilege? The most frequently discussed kinds of privilege in the United States are racial, gender, and socioeconomic, but there are also privileges based upon religion, sexual orientations, and gender identity. Let's think about the top three layers of privilege in the USA.

The first layer of privilege in America is being white. Being white is simply more convenient and more protected than being a person of color in America. Being white has a statistical advantage in gaining employment, getting home loans, getting car loans, and being able to do all these things under more favorable conditions such as being paid the highest rate of income, and being charged the lowest interest rates when compared to statistically similar counterparts of other ethnic groups (with same incomes and credit scores). This is known as white privilege. White privilege is systemic favor, advantage, or "head start" (often financially) that one gets simply because they're white. While the favor is being extended to white people, penalty is often being extended to people of color, including Black people.

## Systemic Racism

Systemic Racism is the opposite side of a two-sided "coin" with privilege being one side and systemic racism being the other. You can't have systemic racism without it resulting in privilege, and you can't privilege any group for a significant time without it resulting in systemic racism. Privilege is an unearned disadvantage that is built into the systems and institutions. Even in the absence of personal racism, systems work to enforce disadvantages based upon race. Some examples involve red-lining policies, preventing people of color from buying homes outside of Black neighborhoods, creating downward spirals of property values because banks also refused to make home loans inside the "red lined" areas. Another example of systemic racism was the practice of school segregation, promising to be "separate but equal" while the funding for schools in communities of color was greatly reduced when compared to schools in white neighborhoods. Underfunded schools create disadvantages for education, for teacher pay, for school equipment and property upkeep, and for college preparation.

Examples of underserved financial penalties to people of color:

- Check out cases where people paid higher interest rates or were denied loans just for being Black: https://www.ftc.gov/news-events/blogs/business-blog/2020/05/ftc-says-bronx-honda-discriminated-against-african-american

- Or how banks block people of color from purchasing homes:  https://www.chicagotribune.com/business/ct-biz-modern-day-redlining-20180215-story.html

- Learn about the historic practice of redlining from which the modern discrimination cases have morphed: https://www.pbs.org/video/redlining-jim-crow-laws-north/

The second layer of privilege in America is gender. Census Bureau evidence, and as in the example above:

- Men get paid more (for the same work) and have more access to the executive suites in America.

- Men hold most of the positions in law making bodies and judicial bodies at every level in the United States.

- Men have access to the highest incomes and influence with other high-income earners.

- Men are more often lawmakers and enforcers in America.

- Men have more representation in American religious institutions, which have historically had a heavy influence with both lawmaking and judicial bodies, but also in industry.

Even without inherited status or financial resources, a man can grow up poor, have no inheritance or money to start out, and still have an advantage over a woman getting a job they are both similarly qualified for. If those doing the hiring are more "comfortable" working with men or have a bias against women or their abilities in the industry, the man will get the job simply because he's a qualified man. This is known as male privilege. Male privilege is common in historically paternalistic cultures.

The third (and maybe the most advantageous) layer of privilege is socioeconomic privilege. While remembering that privilege is unearned, be mindful that socioeconomic privilege is what one has from being born into wealth and having access to the benefits of wealth BEFORE they earned any of their own. Socioeconomic privilege is experienced by those who have plenty, who in addition to having basic necessities of food, shelter, and clothing met without ever being concerned about whether those things would be available have also had access to private schools, tutors, camps, travel, and other expensive extracurricular activities.

People who have socioeconomic privilege get to take the time to go to college rather than straight to work after high school. They are able to pay tutors to help them with entrance exam scores, may take the entrance exams multiple times, and sometimes even get the help of their parents' donations to be accepted into college (as demonstrated by recent college entrance bribery cases). They may have their college education and advanced degrees paid for by their parents or grandparents.

There are other markers of socioeconomic privilege, such as being given your first automobile rather than having to buy it yourself, traveling abroad for vacations as a child or student (paid by others expense), and having the ability to receive from one's parents financial or legal help in the case of a brush with the law. Less-privileged individuals do not get the cultural experiences of international travel, and if they should have a brush with the law would be reliant on public defenders, who are motivated to take plea bargain deals for their clients. These two examples of travel and financial support affects both experience and income opportunities. The long-term income and employability of a person with any legal conviction is compromised. By contrast, many of these same types of convictions are escaped by privileged young people whose parents have attorneys and friends in places of influence.

Socioeconomic privilege gives people who have it a head start in their own economic "success" in that, while non-privileged students are working during high school and college to support their families and/or pay their own tuition and expenses, privileged students are able to attend more extracurricular activities that create professional networks. Privileged students are also shown to have more time to simply study along with disposable income to hire tutors, so their GPA may help them access even more resources.

Socioeconomic privilege creates opportunities for some students because of the positions of their parents to get "internships" in organizations where they can expect immediate employment and high pay after they leave school. Students without these connections, by comparison, start in lower-paying jobs earning their way from the bottom up.

Racial privilege, male privilege, even socioeconomic privilege are unearned benefits that we inherit or are given which come in various layers that have compounded benefits and protections when layered on top of each other. If a person was to be born with every layer of advantage and insulation (protection), being white, male, inherited wealth, heterosexual, and Christian has historically provided the most favored conditions and "insulation." Such a person has the capability financially, politically, and economically to negotiate the most difficult circumstances, such as having unexpected illness, financial challenges, legal difficulties, or loss of employment. This person has more layers of insulation available to them, not only personally, but with embedded support systems, connections, and allies that were inherited at birth. By being born into the family they were born into, having accumulated for generations the "assets" and networks of favor and insulation, long-term favor is granted to them through the systems of employment, healthcare, and legal entities.

However, it is important to understand that every person who appears to have privilege (because of appearing white or white male, etc.) may not have all the privilege they appear to. Still, because of the appearance of being an "insider," they still have more access and influence than those who do not by the visual evaluation of strangers appearing to "belong." Doors more easily open for the apparent insider than for the obvious outsider.

How does privilege blind us? Privilege keeps us isolated from and ignorant of those who don't benefit from the privileges we assume are standard to everybody.

Defensiveness: The discussion of privilege can trigger people to react defensively because the word alone "privilege" or "white privilege" can feel like an accusation if it is either misused or misunderstood. When anxiety and uncertainty go up, communication effectiveness and communication satisfaction go down. As we've learned, anxiety and uncertainty reduce the chance of successfully communicating, clearing up misunderstandings, and connecting with others. When we have anxiety-filled conversations that don't end well (dissatisfaction), we are likely to avoid them in the future according to the Anxiety/Uncertainty management theory.

"White privilege" is a highly misunderstood and triggering term to those who do not understand its true meaning. People tend to react to the term as if it is an accusation of personal, intentional wrongdoing, or choosing to cause harm to people who do not have privilege. It is not an accusation; it is a sociological term referring to how people at different places in society can expect to be treated. If you happen to be one of those people who is statistically proven to be at the top of the hierarchy, you have probably experienced some preferential treatment that you were not even aware was preferential. You may assume everybody gets a warning when they get pulled over by traffic police.

Limited experiences with people of color: White privilege is in some respects a description of cultural patterns in which white people receive favors and benefits that are often not afforded to Black people and other people of color in the United States. If you are a person of European descent, you may not have noticed it because, much like oxygen, you don't know you have privilege unless it is withdrawn. You may also not realize the extent to which others don't receive the same favors or benefits of the doubt. The reason you may not know is because most of the people of color you know personally are not people who you have close relationships with. In close relationships, we learn of the deeply painful personal experiences of our lives. In close relationships, we listen and feel each other's pain.

Recent examples of white privilege and blindness to the experiences of people of color have been demonstrated by the deaths of Ahmaud Arbery, a Black man jogging (who was assumed to be the suspect in recent robberies in the neighborhood). Another example is the brutal response to a call about a counterfeit $20 bill, which may have been passed unknowingly by the late George Floyd. Neither man was given the benefit of the doubt. Any white person in the same position would have been handled differently, and would probably still be alive.

In recent videos gone viral, white Americans have been able to witness murders of Black men that would be unimaginable to white men in America. In the case of Ahmaud Arbery, he was chased, held at gunpoint, questioned, and shot three times. A second truck driver used his vehicle to block Ahmaud when he tried to escape, and filmed parts of the incident. The local police chose not to press charges, claiming the men who killed Mr. Arbery acted in self-defense. It was only after the video leaked to the public that the public became so outraged that the Georgia Bureau of Investigation looked at the case and pressed charges.

In the case of George Floyd, America watched an excruciating video of a Minneapolis police officer kneeling on Floyd's neck for close to nine minutes after he was handcuffed and subdued, begging for his life, saying he could not breathe, and finally with his last breaths calling out for his deceased mother.

White privilege is knowing you can run through your neighborhood without being assumed to be a criminal suspect. White privilege is knowing that, if you are accused of passing a counterfeit bill, you will get an opportunity to defend yourself, and you can be confident you will survive the arrest. White privilege is not knowing that this has been happening to Black people in the United States since emancipation and even worse before emancipation.

White privilege is that after emancipation Jim Crow laws were passed that prevented Black people from being able to attend colleges, or apply for jobs in the same organizations as white people (where pay was higher and more government resources were spent). Many of the colleges people of color could attend were "trade" schools or "teaching" schools only, limiting the employment to low-paying jobs and jobs in Black schools or communities only.

White privilege is being able to get housing loans in whatever neighborhood you wish to live at lower interest rates than a Black person of the same credit score and income level (research "redlining" and recent judgements against Honda, Wells Fargo, and Bank of America).

White people often do not know they have privileges that Black people don't have because we (or our ancestors) haven't been listening or simply didn't care when we were told.

The worst thing about white privilege is that it makes us blind and ignorant to what is happening to our neighbors, friends, relatives, and coworkers of color. Because of the benefits we have, we are insulated from experiencing the mistreatment of those who do not have those benefits.

Why aren't people willing to put themselves in uncomfortable situations related to race? It's simple – choice and options are available to those in power.

Privilege allows us to choose not to interact with anyone of another "race." Privilege gives you options to choose who to do business with, who to hire, who to avoid in your daily life. Where do you shop? Get your hair cut? Attend religious services? With whom do you work most of the time? People in non-dominant populations have never had that option to choose not to engage with groups outside of their cultural group since they were brought or immigrated to the continental United States.

From the 16th century, and likely before, Africans from many tribes and nations were kidnapped and brought to Europe and the U.S.A. As American slaves, they had to interact with people of another race and another cultural group constantly. Indigenous people groups were similarly displaced and forced to interact outside of their chosen cultural groups. Longtime residents of the southwestern United States (Texas, New Mexico, California, etc.) were forced off their land; their children were shipped to boarding schools which forced "English only" speaking;

and they were robbed of property which had been theirs for generations. This was all done in violation of American treaties (The Treaty of Hidalgo Guadelupe) with Mexico. People of color have been forced to interact and listen to white people since Columbus first landed on these shores.

Domination and colonization have been the norm in the United States which has embedded within it a patriarchal structure empowering white people, mostly males, to avoid the conversation altogether. To further obscure the conversation, holy scriptures were used to justify individual, institutional, and systematic racism creating the intentional lack of equity between people groups.

We have outlined just a few of the ways in which the intentional systems of domination have created a classist system of privileges for some and disadvantages for others.

**These are some of the things that blind us.**

# 7

# BLINDER 5:
# IMMATURITY

## Trauma's effects on maturation

As a nation, we experienced early and ongoing emotional trauma, which created a collective "antisocial personality disorder." In our national development, we became morally stunted and our consciences are seared because of our use of humans for free labor, and the methods required to subdue their free will and God-given identities. Obviously, the responsibility for this lies on the Founding Fathers, and those who have come since who set up the rules and penalty systems, the enforcement of which has promoted the exclusion of human rights for all people of color but especially Black people who were considered either ¼ or ⅗ human (for purposes of taxation and population representation to set up the electoral college respectively). Historically, we counted people who were captive in slavery as partial humans when it benefited the state for taxation purposes of the plantation owners who were profiting off of their labor, or when it benefited the south for more voting representation in the electoral college.

Just as a child who is traumatized may miss some steps of emotional or moral development, so has the United States of America. The good news is, we can engage in some national "therapy," moral development, restructuring, repair, and healing. When we do this as individuals and on local, state, and national levels, we will know we are maturing.

Early childhood trauma can cause us to get "stuck" psychologically (emotional and mental processing) at our developmental age at the time of the trauma. Post-Traumatic Stress Disorder is the aftermath of severe trauma. We know the term best as described by the condition of many veterans coming home from wars, however, PTSD is also a condition that many people who were abused as children suffer. Americans have been traumatized by racial abuse and the resulting triggers and conflict since the nation's inception. Even the offender's soul is damaged by causing the trauma.

Research on human development and behavior has shown us that any experience in our early childhood has an impact on who we become. Areas that remain underdeveloped need to go through the natural developmental process of growing through the stages to bring one to maturity in that area of underdevelopment. In other words, it takes time to mature in an area where we had little to no experience, and it shows up in several different ways. For some, it shows up as overcompensating; for others, it shows up as ignorance or defensiveness; and for some, as attachment disorders and/or antisocial personality disorder. On a collective level, we have a severe diagnosis which requires intervention.

Recent research has found that both individual and group trauma may be passed on at a cellular level to future generations. If we consider the impact of the hundreds of years that spanned the North Atlantic Slave Trade period, which historians agree is the most inhumane practice of slavery that has ever been known, we can only begin to comprehend the damage that has been done to individuals, families, tribes, and nations that were subjected not only to slavery itself, but also to the survivors who have made valiant efforts to rebuild without the benefits of family wealth, land, traditions, histories, or legacy. The trauma has been unimaginable, yet if we look at Black Americans today the words of poet Maya Angelou resonate loudly, "Still, I (we) rise!"

## Growing up into cultural sightedness

A person who has had no encounter with other cultural groups, where their only exposure was to those of the same racial group and community (homogeneous environment) may be confident in who they are and in their world perspective yet be naive as to the larger context of racial tension, triggers and reality of life outside of their cultural context. Their confidence may be simply naive since they only know how the small part of the world where they came from works.

Another group to consider are those who have only experienced life biculturally. In other words, someone who grew up as a Vietnamese male in a predominantly Black neighborhood has an entirely different experience and level of competency in intercultural than a person who grew up primarily with either Vietnamese neighbors or Black neighbors. This is like how both Angela and LaTonya's experiences as children in Europe and the Philippines have contributed to their knowledge, skills, abilities, and willingness to lead difficult conversations about race, and culture.

The point is that personal histories influence our level of comfort and competence in engaging with those from other cultural groups. Any lack of experience or exposure to cultural groups outside of our own elevates anxiety, uncertainty, and the chance of failure, including offensive or divisive behaviors because we fail to understand exactly how to adapt our cultural behaviors which includes communication preferences (such as volume, proximity, touch, silence/pauses, question asking, etc.).

For example, European American women often touch each other's hair as they give a compliment about hair, which is viewed as affectionate and/or sincere. However, in historical context, white people were "owners" and engaged in behaviors of severe abuse and entitlement to Black bodies. This historic context makes it highly offensive and even threatening when white people take any privilege to touch or control Black bodies today. Touching (or even asking to touch) the hair or body of a Black person without permission is not only offensive and rude, but can "trigger painful memories, feelings, and fears called flashbacks." While the intent to compliment and express sincerity might be the same (as touching another white person's hair), the impact is not.

For those having their first misunderstanding or conflict of an interracial nature, recognizing the behavior as culturally immature due to a lack of knowledge opens the opportunity for education and/or training. Being willing to learn and grow, being receptive to correction when we make errors creates opportunity to form relationships. Instead, many people become defensive, discount requests and guidance from members of non-dominant cultural groups and lose relational and growth benefits. Following virtual friends of color, learning, and listening (without badgering) can be a very helpful resource in acquiring some basic cultural maturity.

Consider the impact of your actions, even more than your intent. Across cultural groups, non-verbal behaviors and words have different meanings (touching hair, cheek kisses, terms of affection). It is best to always presume positive intent but consider whether a word or non-verbal choice will hold the same meaning for a person in another cultural group. Unfortunately, some of these lessons are learned the hard way—by making mistakes. When you make mistakes, listen to understand why it's inappropriate, apologize, and commit to doing better to whomever you have offended or hurt.

Those with cultural maturity will focus on gaining understanding to empower, building rather than eroding relationships and trust.

Exposure to people who are diverse from ourselves informs and educates us. A lot of our knowledge and competence regarding race relations is done through informal education. We can make intercultural and interracial contact positive (satisfying) by listening to one another, learning to communicate about our concerns, and paying attention to people's histories or experiences as they understand them. Save "debates" about policy for more mature relationships that are deeply rooted in concern for one another. Build trust and friendship first.

# 8

## REMOVE THE BLINDERS

Now that we have walked through each of the five blinders that can impede our ability to see color, let's look at steps we can take to remove the blinders. The steps include:

- Getting comfortable being uncomfortable
- Immersion into varied cultural context
- Taking responsibility for your own growth and development
- Learning cultural communication preferences
- Recording your thoughts

Each step aids in the journey toward recognition of cultural blinders which will empower you to see color and respect culture and connect and communicate effectively as you build relationship with one another.

## Step 1: Get comfortable with being uncomfortable

Meaning, when we're stretched and when we're uncomfortable, we gain new Knowledge, Skills, and

Abilities (KSAs). A baby never learns to walk without falling; yet, they get up over and over again and they don't let the fear of falling stop them from learning to walk. If they never learn to walk, they will certainly never learn to run.

We are all born with courage. Perhaps as our egos and our power grow, we lose humility and decide that we don't have to enact that courage to challenge ourselves or become intentionally uncomfortable. Perhaps we just get too comfortable, and when growth opportunities present themselves, we run from them.

Perhaps it is that as life wounds us, so we put on more and more armor to protect ourselves. We end up with so much armor (rhetoric, arguments, traditions) that we can barely "move" outside of what is comfortable. Getting uncomfortable requires transparency, vulnerability, and courage. We challenge you to be brave again, take off the armor, and join the adventure of cultural sightedness.

## Step 2: Immerse yourself in cultural experiences

Attend and maybe even become a part of events and organizations that are primarily led by people from outside of your own cultural group. Be intentional about the choice. If you like singing gospel music at your predominantly white church and the new community choir is predominantly American Black, join the community choir. You will broaden your musical skills, repertoire, cultural fluency, and friendship possibilities. Conversely, if you are a Black or Asian male who likes country music, then sing, dance, and play country music. Don't ignore your passion or interests because of fear, broaden them.

Start with something you already like or are good at and find a new community to try it with. If you like to dance, try going to a Latinx club and learn to dance in a new way and a new environment, where you are the "stranger."

We can choose to talk to strangers in the grocery store or we can choose to make connections across the boundaries or barriers that make us uncomfortable. "If you're not intentionally inclusive, you will be unintentionally exclusive[xix]" (Courage, 2008).

## Step 3: Take responsibility for your own growth and development

Teach yourself as much as possible about racial groups and other cultures. Information is readily accessible through Facebook, Google, and Google Scholar. Do some of your own work without putting the burden on people who are in the numerical minority to be your educators or example regarding race or color matters. Let's begin to educate ourselves with the tools available at our fingertips.

---

xix Courage, A. (2008). Classroom Communication.

*Media Literacy:* Most important is to be aware of your own biases and seek information that challenges it. Much inaccurate information is available at our fingertips, so be careful to consider these things when thinking about things you see online (including Facebook posts).

*A. Consider the source:* (ask some questions and do not believe everything you read): Remember that many people make money for exploiting current events, and they cater to a particular audience.

- **What type of organization is providing the information?** If they get paid by advertisers or sponsors their information (or lack of some information) should be viewed cautiously because it may be inaccurate or incomplete. Know what the bias of the organization is and then decide if they are providing credible, balanced information.

- Sources that come from educational (.edu) or government (.gov) institutions are considered the most factual, and statistically truthful. Topic experts who cite sources and references to the information they share are also credible sources. Example: For information about the long term physical and psychological effects of abortion, going to an organization site that promotes choice or is against abortion may get you biased information. You may opt to look for more data-based information in a long-term study of women who have had abortions versus those who made the choice not to have an abortion. Likewise, regarding color and race, the same approach could be considered. The objective to is look for unbiased sources: unbiased sources will tell the whole story; biased sources will only tell the part that benefits their agenda.

- Be cautious of third-party information and commentaries. Look for data references in the information shared. Review the third-person account to determine if they have used data from scientifically gathered polls. This is considered reliable information. The polling agency is held accountable by other bodies to use appropriate methods to gather and report information. This makes it more reliable than 10 phone calls to best friends would be.

*Diversify your sources of information and media:* Every organization needs money to function. The source of this money can cause bias and perpetuate agendas that are not transparent or disclosed. To best understand the news and media, get your information from known sources, and where possible, neutral sources. Seek to learn what you don't know, and what your favorite sources aren't telling you. What groups and people do you feel defensive toward? The answers to these questions are clues as to where you may need to seek more information from less biased sources.

- Balance Fox news with NPR or PBS news see the attached report[xx]

- Balance story and intuition-based reports with fact-based reports

- Follow diverse personalities and listen to perspectives from diverse walks of life: Joel Olstein and TD Jakes can give you a fuller spiritual perspective than one or the other.

- Follow and critically listen to opposites like Don Lemon and Trevor Noah (both Black men who make commentary on current events from opposite perspectives)

- Follow organizations that educate on information you didn't learn in school, perhaps the National African American History Museum could help inform on things you didn't learn when your school taught that the Civil War was primarily about State's rights (most Southern states did this, and Northern states didn't do much better).

*B. Be skeptical of interpretations of statistics* by nonprofessionals and non-experts. If a person is a subject matter expert, they will have a Master's or PhD level education in that field (or comparable work experience in that field). Consider these questions:

---

xx  Relman, E. (2018, June 21). These are the most and least biased news outlets in the US, according to Americans. Retrieved from https://www.businessinsider. com/most-and-least-biased-news-outlets-in-america-2018-6

- What is the expertise of the source?

- What is the motivation or the agenda of the source of information?

- Do they get paid for their opinion?

- Is their information based on fact or opinion? For instance, faculty from validated research institutions produce information and articles that are reviewed by peers before it can be released.

- What is the source benefitting from the information they are sharing?

- What is the bias of the source?

- Is there selective attention and confirmation bias present? Don't search for one unqualified source that holds a view you agree with, be intellectually honest and pay attention to what most experts are saying even if you don't agree

*Defer to the expert:* Would you rather have your taxes done by an accountant or an employee at the local animal shelter? One is an expert on tracking and calculating money, and the other is not. Obviously, you would prefer the accountant. When it comes to matters of racial, cultural, historic learning, trust people who have invested the time, energy, and effort to garner expertise in this specific area.

- For economic advice trust economic experts (listen to experts with diverse views to get best information)

- For organizational policy and procedures, trust the human resource professionals and business partners whose job it is to know, interpret and help hold others accountable for enforcement within the organization

- For racial issues, trust experts with either professional expertise and/or life experiences (preferably both) dealing with racial concerns (historians, researchers, sociologists, scientists, other professional experts, AND people with life experiences negotiating racism are "experts.")

When considering sources, know what the bias of the organization is and then decide if they are providing credible, balanced information and perspective. Recognize and acknowledge that there are some sources who are either paid by advertisers or donors to promote their position or to raise and maintain funding. Evaluate the mission of the group to determine if it is a source that is sharing trustworthy information.

## Step 4: Learn Cultural Communication Preferences

Cultural groups have different preferences for communication when it comes to talking and listening. In large countries such as the United States of America, there are many cultural groups within one larger culture. Where we all may share some cultural "norms," there are still some specific preferences and patterns for each co-cultural group that are a result of our ancestors passing on their own cultural rules and experiences. Most of this "rule passing" happens informally, even unconsciously as we passively learn our own ways with words and non-verbal communication tools from our parents who learned the rules from their parents, who learned the rules from their parents, and so on as far back as before our families first came to the shores of this continent (or were invaded by those who came to these shores).

Every cultural group has both verbal codes (rules) and non-verbal codes. Some cultures prefer speaking directly and explicitly with concern for the clarity of the speaker, while some prefer indirect, face-saving strategies with intentional concern for the feelings and "face" of the audience. Face-saving messages are careful not to cause embarrassment or shame to the individual who is more importantly a group member because public embarrassment to a member would bring group shame[xxi].

Cultures that emphasize attention to and clarity of the (one) speaker are generally *individualistic* cultures, placing responsibility on the individual as both speaker, action taker, and solo identity of accountability as "I." Cultures that emphasize the effect and impact of the message on the (whole) audience most generally have high cultural values for *collectivism*, valuing group action and identity as "we" more than individual identity is emphasized

xxi Cooper, P., Calloway-Thomas, C., Simonds, C. (2007). Intercultural Communication: A text with readings. Pearson Education, Boston, MA.

because INTERdependence and harmony are crucial for meeting group needs and goals which receive preference over individual needs and goals in collectivistic cultural groups.

These are the unwritten contextual rules that members of cultural groups know because we have been trained (socialized) in these groups, but outsiders may not know. This is where many misunderstandings and offenses occur. There are many ways that individualism and collectivism play out culturally, but here we will focus on how they impact speech and non-verbal communication codes.

Verbal codes refer to how we use words. Non-verbal codes refer to every other way of communicating including use of our bodies. According to Orbe and Harris[xxii] (2015), kinesics is the use of hands, fingers, arms, legs, and body posture. Paralanguage, also known as vocalics includes pitch, volume, tone, pauses, sarcasm, facial expression, and even non words like 'um" or "uhhh" which are often used in place of words.

Proxemics is the use of space, meaning how close or far do we place our bodies from each other and what does that use of space mean about the relationship between communicators? Touch, also known as hepatics, can communicate affection, comfort, power, control, and abuse among other things. In summary, in addition to our ways

---

xxii   Orbe, M., Harris, T. (2015). Interracial Communication: Theory into practice (3rd ed.). Sage Publications, Thousand Oaks, CA.

with words, non-verbal ways of communicating include the use of the body to communicate, vocal messages which are communicated in ways other than with words, space, and touch. Each cultural group uses both words and non-verbal messaging in slightly different and easily misunderstood (by other groups) ways.

Because of our various group histories and interactions including those involving immigration and the circumstances of immigration (whether forced, voluntary, or refugee driven), oppression and dominance, privilège and lack, language, religion, etc., we have developed cultural patterns that are easily misunderstood between cultural groups and individuals from differing groups.

**Verbal messages**

- Collective words - In collective groups, words, ideas, even group events are understood as "the best" when they come from more than one person and are participatory from the whole. When the whole group participates collaboratively in both the delivery and support of the message, it increases unity, interdependence, and affirms group identity.

A good example of this is demonstrated well in music of the call and response style that originated out of African tradition and was brought to America[xxiii]. This tradition carries on today in traditional Black music but has also

---

xxiii Jones, E. (2015). Gospel Music: The sound of hope. Redemption Press, Enumclaw, WA.

become popularized in other genres. Excellent examples of call and response music are seen in James Brown's 1968 song, "Say it Loud, I'm Black and I'm Proud"[xxiv] and in the crossover hit of the 1967 "Oh Happy Day"[xxv] arranged by James Hawkins.

Call and response communication can be misunderstood by members of individualistic groups as "interrupting" or "disrupting" the speaker rather than as intended to support, affirm, and participate with the speaker (or singer) in unity and solidarity.

In the United States America, most people of color have collectivistic traditions and histories and have carried those values with them as part of their resilience, strength, and survival. Collectivism is often referred to as "family oriented." It is most easily visible when we see families from collectivist communities bring the whole family to buy the groceries including grandma and baby sister. It is an interesting contrast that some politicized conversations have referred to individualistic groups as having "family values" while not embracing this same "family orientation."

Some of the groups in America (U.S.) who researchers have identified to be collectivistic in orientation are the Marshallese, and many of the Latinx, Asian American and African Immigrant communities (of which there are

---

xxiv  Brown, J. (1968) Say it Loud, I'm Black and I'm Proud. https://www.youtube.com/watch?v=KkjaXyuDKYs

xxv  Hawkins, J. (1967) Oh Happy Day! https://www.youtube.com/watch?v=zXq6fdOXdLg&list=RDzXq6fdOXdLg&start_radio=1&t=81

multiple cultures). Black Americans also tend to be lower in collectivism than the aforementioned groups, but lower in individualism than European Americans[xxvi] (Orbe & Harris, 2015).

African Americans are known to demonstrate values for both individualism and collectivism, individualism when engaging in the activities of personal advancement such as career and individual expression, but collectivism regarding support of family and community. African Americans (as many of the other collectivistic groups mentioned before) behave collectivistically with successes, sharing the financial rewards, and knowledge gained with families and the communities. Keep in mind that collectivism and individualism are a continuum, each being at opposite ends of the continuum. Some groups, families, and individuals may be higher in collectivism than others, depending upon a combination of their group and individual experiences.

See the example below which is by no means exhaustive but simplified to give you an image of the continuum and where some people groups in America operate on the continuum of Collectivism/Individualism.

xxvi  Orbe, M., Harris, T. (2015). Interracial Communication: Theory into practice (3rd ed.). Sage Publications, Thousand Oaks, CA.

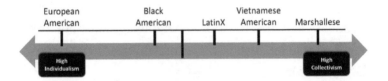

- Many words - Many words (also known as "instrumental style"[xxvii]) often come from individualistic cultural beliefs that it is the speaker's responsibility to be clear, therefore, explanations may be made in multiple ways using alternate words with the message sender's responsibility for clarity in mind. This can be perceived as condescending or insulting of intelligence by members from collectivistic groups (affective communication style-which is receiver oriented). Using many words are often understood as exertions or acts of dominance when not allowing equal space and time for non-dominant groups or individuals to have equal input and/or expression. Keep in mind that individualism/collectivism are a continuum and that some groups, families, and individuals may be higher in individualism or collectivism than others of their same cultural group, depending upon their group and individual experiences.

European Americans tend to prefer data and debate, which is typical of both individualism and instrumental-style communication. Because of this, they engage in

---

xxvii  Cooper, P., Calloway-Thomas, C., Simonds, C. (2007). Intercultural
       Communication: A text with readings. Pearson Education, Boston, MA.

debate and argumentation, "which is a cultural tradition stemming from the Greco-Roman Aristotelian method." While this method emphasizes that the best information will rise to the top and the best ideas will become public policy, it is not the most effective method for gaining understanding of relational partners from other cultural traditions, or for intimate relationships with similar cultural partners.

People of European-American descent should be mindful that while the crucible of "argument" of ideas to run a society may be of some benefit in the public context, the verbal behavior of "debating" a person's experiences and the meaning of those experiences to them is not only poor listening, but also sends a very dismissive and condescending relationship message.

- Space - Cultural groups tend to see distance as having a message about the concern for the other person . . .or lack of concern.

    - Collectivistic cultural groups often have a closer distance for communication than individualistic cultures. Remembering that collectivistic cultures emphasize the "we" makes it easy to see why it is more "natural" to be in a "we" space physically than a "me" space for members of collectivistic cultures. Members of collectivistic cultures have been raised from birth to be together at all times and are rarely in a room or house alone. When members of collectivistic cultures speak, they are often within 12" of space with each other. This sends a message of closeness and concern about the other person. This closeness can be misunderstood by individualistic cultural members as "invasive, lacking respect, and without personal boundaries."

- Individualistic cultural groups have been socialized since birth as "I" rather than as part of a "we." Therefore, individualistic cultural groups often are expected by their families to "self soothe" and to function independently (often without assistance) as a sign of "maturity." Because of the emphasis on independence, space is also expected. This is demonstrated by the 36" rule, where members of individualistic cultures often require most people, to stay a distance of at least 36" away from each other person's "personal space." This can be misunderstood by members of collectivistic cultural groups as "cold, distant, or rude."

People from individualistic groups often misinterpret the closeness (physically and emotionally) with family of collectivistic people as "codependent." This is an ethnocentric bias, believing that "my cultural ways are best." People from collectivistic groups can feel neglected or that the commitment of friends and family from individualistic cultures is lacking because "space" (either physical or emotional) is not an element of high value in collectivistic cultures, whereas it is in individualistic cultures.

## Touch

* Touch - can be understood and even intended in multiple ways. Research shows that men often touch women's bodies in seemingly (to them) non-sexual ways that are unwelcome and experienced by women as attempts at ownership and dominance.

During the Biden vice presidency and campaign, several stories of what may have seemed to him like "fatherly" touches or hugs of women and girls on their shoulders, backs, etc. demonstrated a paternalistic entitlement to women's bodies even in professional contexts. (This is an example of a cultural conflict that has been raging for ages between the cultural groups of males and females.)

Similarly, interracial touch can be just as unwelcome and feel even more entitled and invasive than inter-gendered touch. Black women report often being asked or not even asked by white strangers and acquaintances if "I can touch your hair." Given the history of dominance and oppression of Black bodies, in addition to dominance and historic abuse of Black female bodies, this is a highly offensive and threatening practice from anyone outside of the Black community, even those who consider themselves to be "friends."

Touch (as with all communication) is contextual. Hand holding in many collectivistic cultures is a sign of friendship, and has no sexual meaning, even between two people of the same sex. A kiss on the cheek is considered a friendly greeting between family and friends in many European cultures, but also among Latin Americans and in the Middle East. Public displays of romantic love may be heartwarming at a wedding celebration but are discouraged by the water cooler at work.

## Vocalics

- Vocalics - Use of voice including volume, vocalizations, and non-word utterances vary. To many collectivistic groups, increased volume means excitement and happiness, while to European Americans, volume often signals anger and threat.

Pitch of voice has specialized meaning as well. When the pitch at the end of a sentence goes down, that pitch may be interpreted as a "condescending tone" whereas when the pitch goes up it may be perceived to be a message of surprise, interest, or even of excitement.

The difficulty is that like the other methods of communicating, we often don't speak the same "tone languages." The downward tone may mean boredom instead of condescending attitude. The upward pitch could also mean irritation rather than excitement. When one is mistaken for the other, we misjudge one another's intentions and fail to interpret messages correctly. As with other forms of communication, it is necessary to remind ourselves that when crossing cultural boundaries to engage in friendships, we must be aware that things such as tone of voice do not mean the same thing across cultural groups, so we must not assume that our assumption about the other person's intent is correct. It is better to assume that we could be misunderstanding and simply pose questions such as, "How are you feeling about this topic we're discussing?"

- Silence - The term "awkward silence" is an indication of European American preference for words, lots of words, and constant words. However, many cultural groups see silence differently. For Native Americans, silence can mean active listening, ambiguity, or respect[xxviii]. Other collectivistic groups have also been shown to use silence as a form of disagreement, objection, or respect depending on the context. Being a member of the culture helps one to understand the meaning, being an "outsider" makes it more likely to misunderstand the meaning of this and other ways of expressing human thought and feeling in cultural contexts.

Students studying in the USA from Japan, China, and other Asian countries often find it very difficult to adjust to being asked to speak in the American classroom for multiple reasons. First of all, volunteering to talk in the

---

xxviii Nakane, C. (1984). The social system reflected in the interpersonal communication. In Condon, J., Saito, M. (eds.). Intercultural encounters with Japan. Tokyo: Simul Press.

class is not associated with higher intelligence but with lack of self-control, thoughtful silence is valued, and both Japan and China have cultures that consider the expertise of the Teacher to be much more valuable than any participation the students may bring (this is known as high power distance, where a position such as teacher is one to be highly respected).

For satisfying interpersonal relationships, it is important to consider context. To know what to do and when, it may be best to first understand the overall cultural context and work your way down to the individual (when in an organizational context). When the most important thing is to understand an individual in an interpersonal relationship, it may be best to start with the individual and their cultural context, then work your way up through the organizational layers in which you may be interacting .

The United States of America as a whole, according to research conducted by Gerte Hofstede[xxix], tends to value individualism; however, within many micro-cultural groups there are higher values for collectivism but among descendants whose ancestors came from Europe, there is a higher value for individualism according to research conducted by multiple researchers in recent years looking at cultural groups within the United States[xxx]. If we

xxix Hofstede, G. (2001) Culture's Consequences: Comparing values, behaviors, institutions, and organizations across nations (2nd ed.). Sage Publications, Thousand Oaks, CA.

xxx Orbe, M., Harris, T. (2015). Interracial Communication: Theory into practice (3rd ed.). Sage Publications, Thousand Oaks, CA.

consider that our families and cultures have largely been segregated until the past 50 years, it is easy to understand how Hofstede[xxxi] found a preference for individualism among Americans.

Assimilationist goals of the founders (the dominant group of European Americans who have held power in every aspect of culture, economics, politics, and even religion) have been enforced. Those in positions of power throughout American history were able to see that their preferences were the ones that were "normalized." History substantiates the common subjugation of cultural ways other than those of the dominant group, with particular cruelty in regard to First Nations people and those who were brought involuntarily during the North American Slave Trade and their descendants. Despite efforts to subjugate and crush non-dominant cultures, most have thrived even when forced underground. For these reasons, it is even more valuable to learn and appreciate the cultural values and expressions of co-cultural groups because of the resilience and lessons the culture has to teach us all.

Many collectivistic (we oriented) cultural groups such as African Americans and Latinos tend to value lived experience and familial relationship over data-driven debate. So experiential evidence carries as much if not more weight with most people of color in the United

---

xxxi  Hofstede, G. (2001) Culture's Consequences: Comparing values, behaviors, institutions, and organizations across nations (2nd ed.). Sage Publications, Thousand Oaks, CA.

States than research or data. One reason for this is that "research" has often overlooked the Black experience, and/ or been conducted through Eurocentric lenses and biases. Thus, debate over the latest findings from the National Bureau of Statistical Nonsense on crime rates is not nearly as applicable as what has happened in our community.

For example, many statistics that are reported from local community level organizations (for example, policing) may not be accurate in that there is no oversight in what incidents get excluded from reports to federal agencies. Take, for example, the recent decisions by local Georgia police and district attorneys to make no charges or arrests in the Ahmaud Arbery death by three white men while Arbery was running through his neighborhood on a Sunday afternoon. Initially, they cited their rights to make "citizen's arrest" because they thought he was a "suspect" then they claimed "self-defense" when Arbery "refused to comply" with their commands in their reports to local police. Their claims were readily accepted, and no charges were filed until the video went viral.

Another example is the death of George Floyd when a Minneapolis police officer inhumanely kneeled on his neck for almost 9 minutes until his life was gone. Incidents such as this have long gone unseen and unreported and thus are underrepresented in "research" and official reports. Local police departments before the oversight of cell phone videos and the Freedom of Information Act have not been likely to self-report on their own misbehavior; thus, there is much information that the public has not had access to unless listening and being present in communities of color.

Communities of color tend to be collectivistic. The reason for this is because it was part of their ancestral history and in part because of the history of oppressive state-endorsed violence and misinformation in the United States. As a result, collectivistic communities of color trust known information from within the community more than data and statistics from outside sources. Statistics and data is known to be incomplete and/or manipulated by dominant powers, and not reflective or inclusive of the experiences of people of color.

Relationships that place a higher value on preferences and thoughts of one person over the other (male over female, white over Black, one culture over another) are doomed to be short term, unsatisfying relationships. If we wish to build relationships and friendships that last and honor each other, we must intentionally listen without "debate" of the other person's experiences and perceptions of "the way things are around here." Problem solving is another style of communication which may require debate, however, make sure to understand the context of when both parties are agreed on "problem solving" vs. relational communication.

Recognize that our own experiences, while true to us, are partial at best, and may not represent all "truth." Here's an example: a man may have a bias against women because he was abandoned by his mother. His perception of women may be mistrustful; however, it may not represent the "truth" about all women (his conclusion that women can't be trusted). Remember that our experiences and passive learning (what we heard our parents and others say) have "colored" our perceptions in such a way that what we "see" or "don't see" may not be factually accurate.

Our engagement across cultural lines is based on how our perceptions were framed during dinner table discussions or in reaction to the news clips, etc. Many of those perceptions have simply been misinformed. It is important to note that the news, print, and entertainment media even before the age of television and film have historically misrepresented people of color in stereotypical ways that maintained hierarchies of dominance and appealed to majority (white) audiences. "Racial/ethnic representation are present through invisibility, stereotyping, or strategic programming and play some role in shaping how people come to understand race relations... presence or absence of each portrayal either advances or stunts the struggle towards interracial understanding. . . because the media play a central role in how persons come to understand self and others"[xxxii] (Orbe & Harris, 2015, p. 293).

What is the "right way"? The best way is the way created together when all relationship partners get to have a voice in deciding "how we want things to be around here." The

xxxii Orbe, M., Harris, T. (2015). Interracial Communication: Theory into practice (3rd ed.). Sage Publications, Thousand Oaks, CA.

longest-lasting relationships that report "satisfaction" meet the needs of both parties according to studies on long-term happily married partners. This is true of romantic couples, but it is also true of lasting friendships and organizations with low turnover. When an organization is being respectful and sensitive to the cultures, traditions, and needs of its members, workers tend to report higher levels of satisfaction which is shown in retention statistics. Dissatisfied workers look for alternate options with better conditions that meet more of their needs as a whole human being.

Cultural Contracts Theory[xxxiii] poses that co-created agreements that are fully negotiable between parties with the only limits being personal preferences validates all parties and cultures. These co-created relationship agreements are motivated out of mutual satisfaction and respect, not historic norms, obligations, or who holds the most power. When engaging in relationships of any kind across cultural, ethnic, and racial lines, co-created agreements bring the most satisfaction, which leads to retention of the relationship, be it employee, neighbor, or friend.

Cultural competence, communication tools, and interpersonal competence help us to bridge the myriad of complexities to consider when engaging outside of the groups in which we have been highly socialized.

---

[xxxiii] Jackson R. (2002a). Cultural Contracts Theory. Toward an understanding of identity negotiation. Communication Quarterly, 50, 359-367.

No person fits perfectly in any group. Each individual has multiple identities and experiences. Most people in the United States are exposed to more than one cultural group. However, people of color have been required to be bicultural and multicultural out of necessity. People of the dominant group in any culture (white people in the USA) can lag behind in cultural competence. The fact that you are reading this book indicates that you have some cultural intelligence and are growing in competence no matter where your cultural story began.

## Step 5: Record your thoughts

Put yourself in a context where you are a participant of the non-dominant population. Newcomers to any culture can see the culture they are suddenly immersed in clearly, but also make observations about their own culture that they have never noticed. The goal here is to create an opportunity for you to understand the experiences of "outsiders" more clearly. Jane Elliott[xxxiv] created this opportunity for her students with the "blue eyes, brown eyes" experiment. After the exercise, individuals took the time to reflect on what it felt like to be an "outsider". Consider whether you feel like you are under a spotlight, being hyper-examined, what your emotional states are, others perceptions and judgments of you and yours of them that may have occurred during the experience. Write

---

xxxiv  Elliott, Jane. (2019). Jane Elliott. Retrieved from https://janeelliott.com/.

about it in a journal, or a social media post *(#seecolorr)*, or in an email to seecolorr@gmail.com.

Make yourself a "minority" so that you can become more emotionally and functionally intelligent about the experiences of those in the numeric minority. Capturing the experience in writing may help you to resonate and relate better with members outside of your own group. You may also find similarities for which you were unaware. There is an old proverb, "Walk a mile in a man's moccasins before you judge him." Judgement is the ability to separate into parts and choose the good[xxxv]. When we exercise our ability to feel what others feel, then we get the right to judge. Many of us are judging without having taken the journey.

When you put yourself in a place to become more empathetic and functionally intelligent about how difficult it is to be the only person of your type in a space, it will help you learn communication and relationship skills necessary to building trust and connection with diverse others.

Every relationship is built on the blocks of communication. So, the quality of your relationships is dictated by the quality of your communication. If you have poor quality or low quantity of relationships with members of particular cultural groups, it is either because you have low access

xxxv  Murner, L.T. (2010). The Rock of Northwest Arkansas.

to that group in your community or because the quality of your communication is poor and your attempts to engage across the color line may be of an insignificant quantity and poor quality. It is common to give up when we make mistakes so keep trying and learning.

You have some new information and tools now, so, please, TRY AGAIN!

# 9

# CONCLUSION

## BEGIN AGAIN

Let's go back to the beginning, before we were afraid. Do you remember when you were a child and had no knowledge about the difference in race and your only knowledge of color had to do with crayons? You might walk up to someone whom you found interesting and simply say "Hey, I want to be your friend!" This is the concept of the beginning that we are describing: a time where we immerse ourselves in environments that allow us to cultivate relationships, fellowship, and create fond memories together that we can reflect upon for years to come.

Grown up relationships are more complicated than those of our childhood because we have more responsibilities to society, and we have made errors that make us cautious or fearful. While we need the innocence of childhood to initiate positive relationships, we also need to be learners ever growing from the perspectives of those who have different experiences than our own to help us know HOW to build those relationships.

We have been programmed with messages from a variety of sources, and, in those messages, we are inundated with the concept of the scary "other." It is part of our brain's needs to "categorize" information and objects in order to process information to sort ingroup members and outgroup members in initial encounters. When combined with fear or biased socialization of outgroup members, humans tend to justify doing harm to "outsiders" more easily.

Context changes the way we need to build each relationship. For instance, when meeting a potential romantic partner or spouse, we pay close attention to their preferences, perspectives, and ideas. We may have entirely different experiences with being preferred (or not) in our jobs, by our families, by our educational institutions, etc. Because of these different experiences, we see the world around us with different "filters" and interpretations. Because of these differences, we need to be intentional to learn how to be good relational partners to each other in various contexts.

Building interracial and intercultural friendships are much the same. As members of different racial/ethnic groups, we have experienced different treatments, which creates different sensitivities and expertise. Therefore, we must be intentional in learning how to best be friends, colleagues, and neighbors and find ways that the other person wants to be treated, talked to, and regarded.

Where color and culture are seen, valued and respected on all sides, we must recognize that each individual's experience is unique and yet, we are each members of groups, some of which have not historically received parity in treatment.

## In the media

Consider the buzz that occurred around the movie Black Panther - did you ask, "Why all the hype?" It was one of the first big box office films that had a cast with leading roles filled with Black actors of strength versus depictions of servitude. In this movie, people from Africa were not depicted as desolate or slaves in need of a white savior. The leaders were Black, responsible, and loving toward one another—and had customs to challenge processes that were unjust to which everyone in the land agreed. That said, there were many who opted not to see the movie because they objected to the dominance of Black actors and chose to see it as "prejudice against white people."

This reasoning dismisses the fact that white people have been the lead actors in movies since cinema inception and even played the role of Black people using blackface, depicting them primarily through the lens of white people. During the early days of reconstruction and silent movies the smash hit, "Birth of a Nation[xxxvi]" (1915) featured the

---

xxxvi Griffith, D., Aitken, H., (1915) Birth of a Nation. https://www.britannica.com/topic/The-Birth-of-a-Nation

plot of a "savage" Black man in pursuit of white virgin to rape her. The actor representing the Black "predator" was a white man in blackface.

Historically, most media in the United States has represented the thoughts and lives of white writers, white actors depicting white plots, experiences, themes, and culture. When a villain was required in the film, many times it was cast to represent a Black person by a white person in blackface; or, as time progressed, a person of color, most often a Black man. "Black Panther" is a story told from the African perspective about African values, tribes, communities, customs, and cultures. The fact that mostly Black people are the cast, directors, and writers makes sense. This is not prejudice, or even discrimination any more than making a movie about the women's suffrage movement and casting mostly women would be prejudiced.

We cannot choose the color of skin that we are born with nor can we change it. Our lack of exposure reflects our immaturity and makes conversations and conflict involving race seem taboo, unsolvable problems. However, if we take the time and energy to remove the barriers of color and actually get to know the person who looks different, what we might find is that which makes us uncomfortable is actually the thing that would help us solve problems together. The answers to what we need are within one another—not individually but collectively.

Imagine an environment where we don't practice self-segregation and rather invest in getting to know others, share our insights, and work together to resolve issues and solve problems. What would be the results?

What holds us back in race relations? It's simple - fear! Really, it's our apprehension that we won't be accepted by the other group or that our perspective about our culture or the value that is placed on our culture and heritage will be diminished by the value of the culture and heritage from others.

Every human wants to be valued for who they are and where they have come from. We want to be appreciated for what we know, what we can do with our skills, and what we contribute to the organizations and families and communities where we spend our time and talents. Being appreciated for our unique abilities and perspectives that are a result of experiences we've had is part of being cared about and appreciated. What is unique about us is often what is the most valuable for group benefits. Nobody wants to be tolerated. Everybody wants to be celebrated.

Remember: when we choose to see color and recognize culture, we have the opportunity to improve our individual world, which enhances our collective world. Choose to SEE COLOR!

We believe we have delivered on our mission with this book to help each reader:

- Reduce stress and anxiety around cultural communication
- Improve confidence about culturally-appropriate dialogue
- Increase capacity to negotiate uncertain contexts
- Become equipped to navigate race and color conversations
- Gain tools to minimize unintentional offense

*You are invited to continue the conversation!*

We want to continue the conversation as this eBook could not exhaust all aspects of the concept of Seeing Color. We invite you to join the conversation and request to join our private Facebook Group (https://www.facebook.com/groups/seecolorr/).

## LEAVE US A REVIEW

We love receiving constructive feedback and we welcome your review of this book as there is more to come. Share your thoughts with us!

Visit our website at seecolorr.com and click the button "Leave Us a Review" to share your thoughts with us.

# ABOUT THE AUTHORS

## Dr. Angela Courage!

Dr. Angela Courage-Mellott (also known as "Doc Courage") holds a Master of Arts in communication with focus in interracial and intercultural communication. Her Doctorate in Higher Education with emphasis in College Teaching and Faculty Leadership empower her as a change agent in the classroom and community.

Dr. Courage Is a sought-after event speaker and educator on interracial & intercultural communication, conflict & faith's role in change, and living out lives of "COURAGE!"

She Is CEO of Courage Communication 4 Change, where she serves as a change agent, empowering students, pastors, church leaders, and the community. She serves as Adjunct Faculty at John Brown University, University of Arkansas, and Ecclesia College in Northwest Arkansas.

Her intentionally multiethnic, multicultural experiences and lifestyle led her to focus studying the science of interracial and intercultural communication, which together uniquely qualify her to lead healthy conversations that empower people to better communicate and connect with diverse others.

Her "Loving Our Neighbors" workshop, is a resource that helps Christian organizations become more representative of the Kingdom of God in policy and practice towards diverse people groups and diversity within local church bodies and the community.

"The quality of your communication dictates the quality of your relationships." (Doc Courage!)

## Dr. LaTonya Jackson

Dr. Jackson is a dynamic, forward-thinking people director who contributes to the ongoing growth of a company, given extensive experience in talent and workforce development, thought leadership, change management, instructional strategy, and facilitation. She is an adaptable, passionate, and goal-oriented human resources professional highly skilled in collaborative partnerships, individual and group coaching, and people development.

Dr. Jackson builds strong interpersonal relationships by utilizing communication skills to connect with colleagues and clients. Improves organizational systems through research-based solutions that perpetuate and augment company revenue results, given a strong work ethic.

Dr. Jackson holds a BSBA in Marketing and Finance from the University of Nebraska Lincoln. She also holds a M.Ed. in Higher Education Leadership and a Doctor of Education in Workforce Development Education from the University of Arkansas.

Dr. Jackson's research focus was on The Self-Efficacy Beliefs of Black Women Leaders in Fortune 500 Companies. She is the author of No Dead Beat Jobs: 7

Reasons Why It's Time to Start Thinking About a Career Change and co-author of I Am Called, a children's book, written with Sydni Jackson.

# Want to Work with Us?

### Speaking, Workshops & Training

*Angela speaks on cultural fluency and communication topics such as:*

- Loving Our Neighbors: The Intersection of Race, Culture and Faith
- Interracial and Intercultural Communication
- Relational Communication: Knowing Your Element
- Recovering (your) COURAGE!

*LaTonya speaks on career and leadership topics such as:*

- Career Transitions: From Bored and Bound to Brilliant
- No Dead-Beat Jobs: 7 Reasons Why It's Time to Start Thinking About a Career Change
- The Layoff Lab: 7 Strategies to Navigate a Layoff Successfully
- Leadership Influence and Power

*Angela and LaTonya together speak on color and culture topics such as:*

- Improving Inclusivity in Organizations
- Removing Cultural Blinders

- COLOR2: A Guide to Building Welcoming Communities
- COLOR2 and Cultural Dissonance: Overcoming Racial Communication Uncertainty and Anxiety
- Shift from FIT (Feelings, Ignorance, Triggers) to FIT2 (Feeling, Informed, Transcend, Transformation)

## CONSULTING

- DICE (Diversity, Inclusion, Communication and Equity) Analysis and Strategy
- Inclusive Leadership Development
- Diversity and Inclusion Coaching – Individual and Group

## MEDIA

Interview Angela "Doc" Courage! And/or LaTonya Jackson for your radio, TV show, podcast, or print media. Expect fresh insights with practical application for your audience. Contact: **seecolorr@gmail.com**